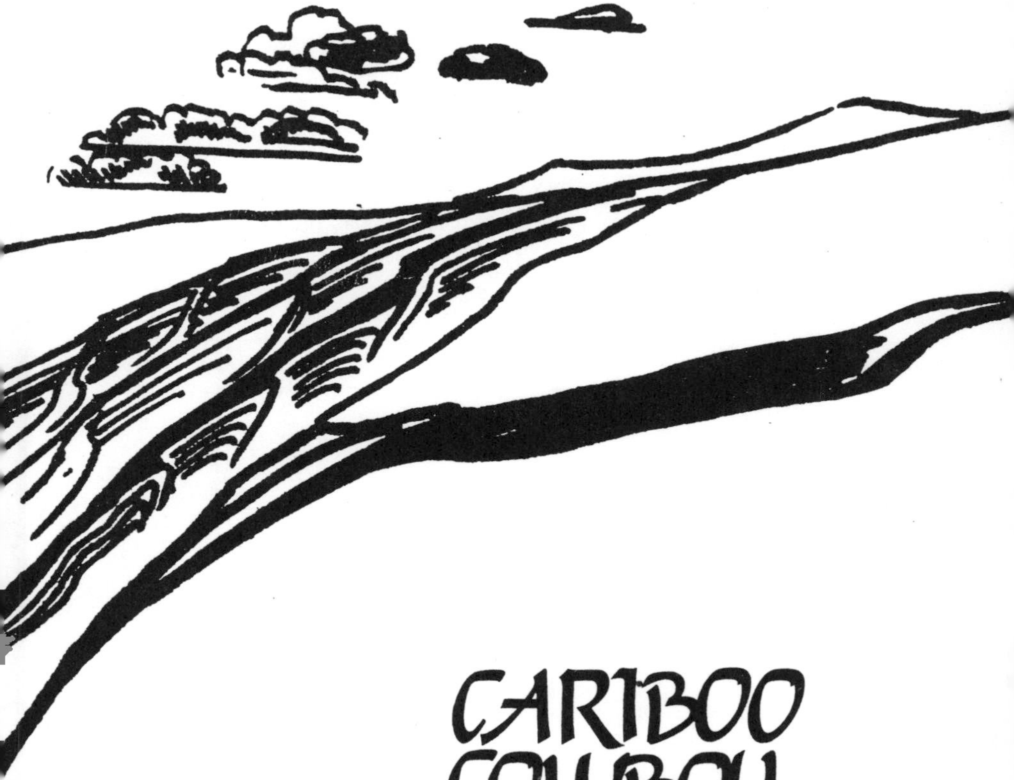

CARIBOO COWBOY

by

HARRY MARRIOTT

W9-CRA-180

FRONT COVER
The author's first job in the Cariboo was on the Gang Ranch, shown on the bank of the Fraser River near Dog Creek.

The painting is by B.C. artist Peter Ewart. It was commissioned by the B. C. Telephone Company and is reprinted courtesy BC Tel.

Copyright © 1994 Estate of Harry Marriott

CANADIAN CATALOGUING IN PUBLICATION DATA

Marriott, Harry, b. 1891
Cariboo cowboy

ISBN 1-895811-08-2

1. Marriott, Harry, b. 1891. 2. Ranchers — British Columbia — Cariboo Region — Biography. 3. Cowboys — British Columbia — Cariboo Region — Biography. 4. Ranch life — British Columbia — Cariboo Region. 5. Frontier and pioneer life — British Columbia — Cariboo Region. 6. Cariboo Region (B.C.) — Biography. I. Title.

FC3845.C3Z49 1994   971.1'7503'092   C93-091729-4
F1089.C3M37 1994

No part of this publication may be reproduced, stored in a retrieval system, or transmitted in any form or by any means, electronic, mechancial, photocopying, recording or otherwise, without the prior written permission of Heritage House Publishing Company Ltd.

First Edition - 1994

HERITAGE HOUSE PUBLISHING COMPANY LTD.
Unit #8 17921 55th Ave., Surrey, B.C. V3S 6C4

Printed in Canada

Dane Campbell Photo

THE AUTHOR

Harry Marriott and his wife, Violet May, better known to her hundreds of resort guests as "Peg". The cowboy-author died in 1969 at 79. His ashes are buried overlooking Big Bar Lake and the country he knew so well and enjoyed so thoroughly.

Peg operated Big Bar Lake Resort for 43 years. When she sold it she kept five acres and built a home on the shore of her beloved lake. Although she is 94 and lives alone, she notes that she is never lonely, regularly visited by guests she hosted over the years. In fact, several of them so enjoyed their stay that their ashes are buried in the surrounding ranchland.

ILLUSTRATIONS

The artist, Sonia Cornwall, daughter of C. G. Cowan who owned the Onward Ranch near Williams Lake, is the wife of Hugh Cornwall. Both are descendants of pioneer Cariboo cattle ranchers and, with their two daughters and son-in-law, operate the Jones Lake Ranch near 150 Mile House. Here Sonia has a studio and spends most of her time depicting ranch life and Cariboo scenes in both oils and water colours.

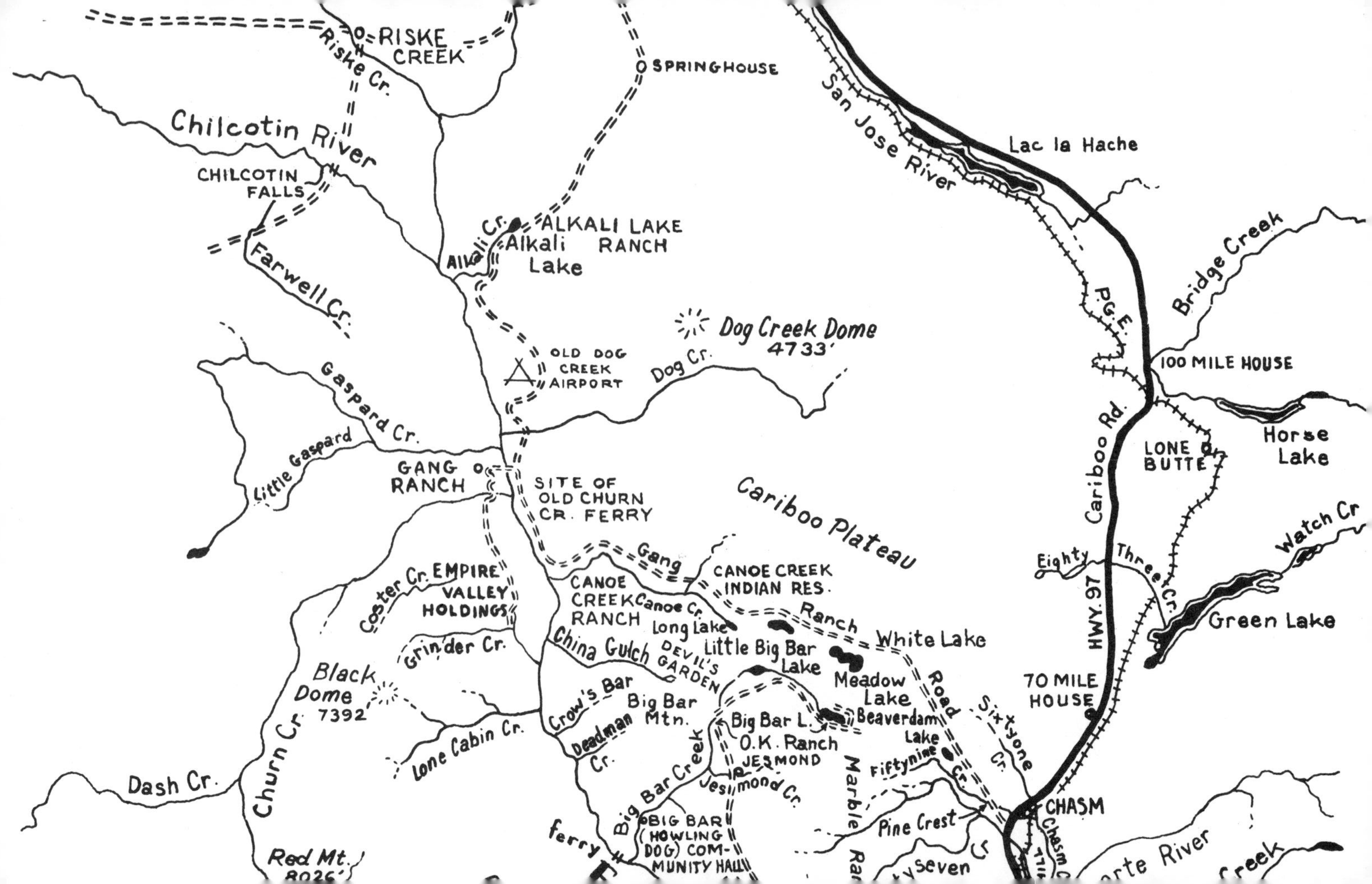
RISKE CREEK
Riske Cr.
SPRINGHOUSE
Chilcotin River
CHILCOTIN FALLS
Farwell Cr.
ALKALI LAKE RANCH
Alkali Lake
Alkali Cr.
San Jose River
Lac la Hache
P.G.E.
Bridge Creek
100 MILE HOUSE
Horse Lake
LONE BUTTE
Cariboo Rd.
Dog Creek Dome 4733'
Dog Cr.
OLD DOG CREEK AIRPORT
Gaspard Cr.
Little Gaspard
GANG RANCH
SITE OF OLD CHURN CR. FERRY
Cariboo Plateau
Gang Ranch Road
CANOE CREEK INDIAN RES.
CANOE CREEK RANCH
Canoe Cr.
Long Lake
Little Big Bar Lake
White Lake
Meadow Lake
Beaverdam Lake
Eighty Three Cr.
Watch Cr
Green Lake
HWY. 97
70 MILE HOUSE
Coster Cr.
EMPIRE VALLEY HOLDINGS
Grinder Cr.
China Gulch
DEVIL'S GARDEN
Black Dome 7392
Crow's Bar
Big Bar Mtn.
Deadman Cr.
Big Bar L.
O.K. Ranch
JESMOND
Jesmond Cr.
Marble Ra
Fiftynine Cr.
Sixtyone Cr.
Lone Cabin Cr.
Churn Cr.
Dash Cr.
Big Bar Creek
BIG BAR (HOWLING DOG) COMMUNITY HALL
ferry
Pine Crest
Seven Cr
CHASM
Chasm C
Red Mt. 8026'
River
Creek

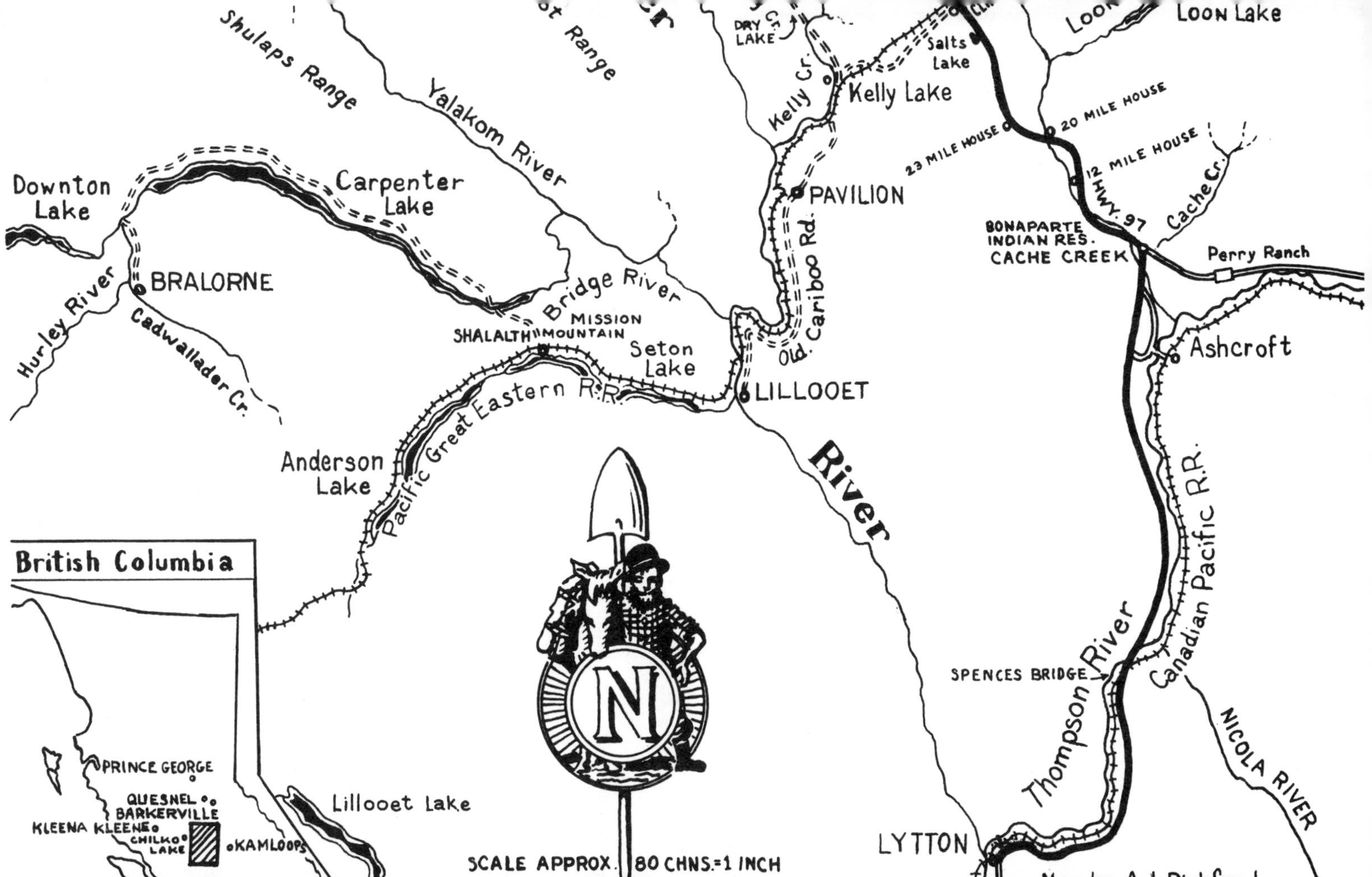

Map by A.J. Pickford

Foreword

I WENT TO THE Big Bar country first in 1922 to teach in the one-room log school down the creek a few miles from Jesmond. Like Harry Marriott ten years earlier, I drank some Fraser River water at Big Bar Ferry, the effect of which persists to this day. Next year after the Neas family pulled out leaving five empty desks in the little school, I began a two-year stint with Cree-speaking pupils in the Peace River Country, after which that Fraser River thirst-quencher compelled a return to Big Bar Creek for another year. Those four years' savings then financed a continuation of my studies, which led to a life very different from Marriott's, and at times far afield. I cannot claim mine has been one whit better than Harry's, but having drunk of the Fraser River in our youth, I share with him an abiding love for the Big Bar Country and its People.

The locale of *Cariboo Cowboy* is one of the most scenic in British Columbia. On summer evenings, sitting on the porch of his lonely Crows Bar cabin, Harry saw the sweep of the Fraser River, nature's primordial artery of the Cariboo, intermittently hidden below the rim of intervening benchlands falling away in the foreground. On the far side, accentuated by shadow-relief, the facing benches rise in thousand-foot steps, a grand fantasy of erosion — remnants of enormous silt deposits laid down in slackened waters of the river, temporarily plugged somewhere downstream by colossal disruptions of the Ice Age. Behind the far benchlands rise buttressed slopes of flanking mountains which, from the Crows Bar viewpoint, are parted by the gap of Lone Cabin Creek to offer a farther vista to the Black Dome, over 6,000 feet above the river, in purple silhouette against the limpid amber-green of sunset.

Below the level of Harry's cabin, the seductive anatomy of this grand amphitheatre is clothed only with sagebrush, greasewood, bunchgrass and cactus. Above, in cooler, moister air is a transition to forest. Higher still, clumps of balsam fir give way to alpine meadows. Above all are the high peaks, like Black Dome, in austere isolation.

The country east of the Fraser also rises steeply from the base level of a thousand feet, to the Cariboo Plateau between three and four thousand feet, a patchwork of meadows, fir-pine thickets, and glistening lakes. Parts like "The Devil's Garden" lying between upper Big Bar and Canoe Creeks are strewn with erratic boulders. Streams draining the plateau drop rapidly into deep-cut valleys as they hurry to join the Fraser River.

Of primary appeal in *Cariboo Cowboy* are the author's treatment of human beings which colour its pages, and his appreciation of those pioneer families of mixed blood. Simon Fraser wrote (1808), "One of the Indians brought in a pistol which Mr. Quesnel lost yesterday.... This was a piece of honesty we did not expect, ... though many things were left loose and scattered ... to afford the natives plenty of opportunities, nothing went astray ... therefore, (they) are more honest than any other tribe on this side of the mountains." In other ways Fraser affirmed the high character of the tribes along his river. Their blood, blended with that of original pioneers such as Grinder, Haller, Bishop, Kostering, Pidgeon, Koster, Murdock, Chisholm, Hartmann, and given a further "stir" with each succeeding generation, produced a virile, colourful, charming, and lovable people. I recall them whooping it up in the Howling Dog Hall (which I helped to build), ample room for three squares on the floor; compulsive rhythm from bow and string by Johnny Grinder, Mrs. MacDonald, and Neil Darrough; Johnny Kostering calling with "inspired" eloquence; babies asleep on overcoats piled at one end of the hall; old-timers on benches around the walls, and pretty girls waiting invitations to dance. Outside, in the frosty air, Sandy Bandhauer brewing gallons of coffee over a bonfire; muffled chuckles from odd males prodding snowbanks for their crocks of "moonshine"; and tied to wagons in the deepening gloom, horses munching hay, awaiting daylight for the long trip home. Past midnight, at refreshment time, one dare not refuse cake or sandwiches made and offered by the local maidens; Harry Coldwell would sing "Juanita" or "Just a Song at Twilight," and Ernest Simms a rollicking sea song, "The Good Ship Yakahikidoola."

In this rich setting, the author unfolds *Cariboo Cowboy* — his own story — with captivating truth, simplicity, homespun humour and philosophy.

GERALD S. ANDREWS,
Surveyor-General of British Columbia, retired.

Contents

Dedication

To Mary Squire
and the real good folks who
love the Cariboo

Chapter 1

I Meet Andy Stobie

THE EVENING SUN has just settled down over the mountain and the twilight shadows are just acreeping along, and I'm sitting out on the porch of a little cabin on Big Bar Creek.

I'm smoking my last cigarette for the day, and talking to two city friends of mine that had dropped in to see me.

We're talking a whole pile about our Cariboo, and I'm a telling them some of the doings of days gone by when one of my friends breaks in and says, "Harry, why don't you get some of these things down on paper? I know a lot of folks who would like to hear some of this old Cariboo."

I got meditating on this some, and though I knew I was no real hand at a lot of words of polite grammar, and not too good with the old pen and ink, yet the idea still hung up pretty regular and often in my old bald head, so I decided I'd make a try and write of the old days, the fine old characters I'd met and worked and rode with, a good class of folks, who'd always feed you and make you welcome when you came riding along. The kind of folks that don't care a damn what you are or how much you've got — just so long as they figured you had the make-up of a real man.

I can tell you of a great rugged type that took everything as it came, good or bad, and never one bit of whining, and of the big wide outdoors, the good fat cows and their white-faced calves on the range, the green grass and the timbered mountains, the lonesome howl of the coyote, and the loud plop of the big trout as he jumped at flies twittering around on Big Bar Lake, and the calm, peaceful sundowns in our "God's Country."

Well, let 'er buck cowboy — time is running out and I'd better get on with my tale.

It was a bright clear morning on May 28 in the year of our Lord 1912 when I stepped out of the Canadian Pacific train at Ashcroft, which at that time was the gateway and main starting off point for the great north country reaching out as far as Fort George, afterwards named Prince George, and to the many points and sparsely settled ranches and homesteads which were tributaries of the great Cariboo Road. This road was the life-blood artery of this whole massive area, which lay east and west for over two hundred miles.

At this time Ashcroft was a one-street village with buildings principally of lumber construction. It consisted of a hotel where good meals were served, and a bar where beer and hard liquor were handed out and sold to the thirsty, of which there seemed to be absolutely no shortage. There was a livery barn which accommodated the strings of freight teams which plodded up and down the Cariboo Road, hauling supplies of all kinds and description to many points in the Upper Country, with high-wheel freight wagons and white canvas covers, spread over ox-bow loops, which kept out rain and dust from supplies.

Ashcroft also had a bank, called the Bank of British North America, which in after years was taken over by the Bank of Montreal. The village also boasted two general merchandising stores and a store owned by a Chinaman named Wing Wo Lung, but most of the supplies came from a good-sized store called Harvey and Bailey, which did a busy farflung trade amongst ranchers for miles around.

At the east end of Ashcroft were dozens of lumber shacks, all sorts and sizes, mostly occupied by Chinamen whose main source of living was growing vegetables, principally potatoes.

In those years the famous BX Stage used to have its headquarters in Ashcroft and every day a smart trotting, four-horse team and stagecoach left Ashcroft for points as far north as Prince George, carrying passengers and mailbags loaded for Clinton, 100 Mile, 150 Mile, Quesnel and Prince George and points along the road. The old BX Stage rolling along presented a very striking picture with its good turnout of equipment. This famous old stage line was noted for its efficiency and dependability in all its transportation business.

I had been away from our British Columbia for a little over two years and had been working on a horse and cattle ranch in Central Washington State, but the call of the North and the urge to see unknown places kept ever whispering to me, and I knew the right place to start for our Cariboo, in those days, was at Ashcroft.

I walked over to the Ashcroft Hotel and being hungry went in to the dining room and wolfed down a big feed of ham and eggs, strong coffee and a stack of hotcakes and syrup piled high on a plate. Having paid for my breakfast I walked out into the main sitting room of the hotel and sat down on one of the vacant chairs, looked around and sized up what sort of a layout I had landed into.

The hotel was a busy beehive full of freight teamsters, all of them four- and six-horse skinners, with the odd eight-horse teamsters. Mostly all of these "boys" were in the process of loading supplies on to their freight wagons for delivery to the many spots along the Cariboo Road.

I didn't notice much liquor drinking in the morning, but I did see considerable bending of elbows as night-time arrived. While I was sitting in the hotel, meditating on this and that, a freckle-faced man with square shoulders and large frame, with light brown hair and sand-coloured mustache, came walking into the hotel. He passed by, looked at me and stopped, and spoke to me in a broad Scotch accent.

"Say, my monny, would you be looking for a job by any chance?"

I replied that I sure was looking for a job. So sitting down on the next chair he asked me where I came from, and what I could do. Had I ever worked on a ranch? I told him that I had come to British Columbia, an immigrant boy from England in 1907, five years earlier, and that I had just returned from Washington two days before. I said that I was very conversant with most forms of ranch life, and I wanted a steady job and a chance to take roots in this big interior and make good.

In this manner I became acquainted with, and became a lifelong friend of, the great Andy Stobie who at that time, and until his death in 1921, was the manager of the famous Gang Ranch and its widely scattered enterprises.

Andy Stobie told me to be ready the next morning to start out for the Gang Ranch, which was 103 miles from Ashcroft, and I was to travel up there with the Gang Ranch freight team, with the driver Mac Haynes. My job would be to help him hook up the four-horse team and help look after them on that long trip ahead — the freight load consisting of flour, tea, coffee, sugar and general supplies for the Gang Ranch. I remember the total load weighed around six thousand pounds.

Stobie made me known to Mac Haynes, a short stocky little man. I walked up to the livery barn with Mac and had a look at the four-horse Gang Ranch team and the freight wagon, already loaded up so there would be no delays in the morning.

As the day drew on I walked around Ashcroft's street, sizing up and listening to the long line skinners' tales; what they had done and what they could do. After having a real man-sized supper at the hotel, I struck off to bed at nine, despite the noisy and jovial elements in the bar-room below me. I remember thinking before I fell asleep that I was really off to a fair start towards that huge and widespread country of the Cariboo.

The next morning, which was May 29, 1912, I woke up with the bright warm sun shining through my window. When I had my clothes on I started up the street to the livery barn and found that Mac Haynes had just got there, so we watered up the team, fed them some hay and oats, threw the harness on them and with this done we went back to the hotel and proceeded to take on another good feed of ham and eggs, coffee and the usual stack of "hots" smothered in syrup.

Mac was in a good pleasant humour and he and I exchanged experiences. The more he talked, the more it seemed to limber up his tongue real well and I gathered that he figured he was a pretty good all-round man, and that he was almost indispensable to the Gang Ranch operation.

However, I figured I'd find out pretty soon how good he was, as I had already had some experience with real good men on ranches, and also with blowhards and bullshitters as they are called in the Cariboo.

We struck up the street after breakfast, proceeded to hook up the four-horse team to the already loaded wagon and both climbed up on the high seat; Mac, of course, on the right side as he was the driver and myself on the left side.

The horses looked like four real good work horses, all of them Clyde stock; the leaders were a good pair of bay mares, called Maude and Queen, while the team on the wagon tongue were called Farmer and Dan. All of them were branded with a JH on their left shoulder, which is the Gang Ranch brand.

Mac kicked the brake loose and we started off and crossed the fast-running green Thompson River on an old wooden bridge at the east end of Ashcroft. We climbed a slow even grade for a mile or so and then you could see the hill was getting steeper every few yards. It took us over three hours to climb that Ashcroft hill and of course the team had to have lots of stops in climbing that steep grade with three tons of supplies on the wagon.

Every freight wagon had good brake blocks on the hind wheels and a little round block, called the chuck block, which was tied by a little chain to the axle. Whenever the wagon stopped the hind wheel was blocked from rolling backwards by this little chuck block.

The country around Ashcroft looked very dry to me, with fairly steep slopes to the Thompson and Bonaparte Rivers. It looked exactly like it was, dry, clay loam and sandy hills, a great deal of it covered with sage brush. The only green vegetation to be seen was on some irrigated fields which looked very green and succulent owing to the fact of being under irrigation from various water sources. This whole area impressed me, in that given enough water it would be quite possible to produce enormous quantities of all agricultural products.

We reached the top of Ashcroft hill and the road ran around a very steep bluff which more or less overhung the Bonaparte River as it boiled along to join the Thompson. It was here on this Ashcroft bluff, in the spring of 1915, that my old friend Henry Koster lost his four purebred bulls which he had shipped from Calgary to Ashcroft. Mr. Koster had a man to drive them to his ranch at Crow's Bar. When these bulls got to the top of the hill at Ashcroft bluff they must have been very hot, dry and thirsty, because when they smelled and saw the water down below them, before the cowboy could realize it, they struck out over the bluff to the water below. Three of them were killed outright, and the fourth bull broke his leg and had to be shot. By a merciful coincidence Mr. Koster had the bulls insured and, luckily for him, the insurance policy on the bulls still had one hour and a half to go before it expired, so Mr. Koster was able to recover the insurance on them.

After Mac and I had passed along the bluff, the road levelled out considerably and the team travelled along in far greater comfort. All around us were sloping hills, with timber on the top of them, which seemed to stretch for miles.

Sitting on the wagon alongside Mac, I gathered a lot of information from him, relative to the Gang Ranch and the various stopping houses we were going to see, and stay overnight at, while we were en route.

We passed by an Indian village, or rancherie as it is called, named the Bonaparte Indian Reserve. There were a considerable number of log cabins and a large white painted church by the side of the road. Around five o'clock we came to a white painted house, with a large-sized barn on the right-hand side of the road.

"Well Harry," Mac said to me, "this is where we are going to stay tonight. This roadhouse is called the 12 Mile House, and a man named Cole MacDonald runs it."

We unhooked the horses, gave them water and hay in the barn and unharnessed them. We then went over to the MacDonald house where we were fed a real good supper. After I had eaten I went out and fed the horses their grain, leaving Mac to talk to a very attractive girl, who I found out afterwards was Cole MacDonald's daughter.

Morning came and around five Mac and I skinned out of bed, watered and fed the team and harnessed up before breakfast. After a good feed we wished the folks goodbye and started on our way, travelling along at a two to three mile an hour gait, up the Bonaparte — the road here was fenced off practically on both sides. We met several freight teams going down towards Ashcroft. The B X Stage en route to Clinton and points north passed us with a flourish and a wave of the hand from the driver, who I afterwards got to know. His name was Fred Peters, and he certainly knew how to handle his ribbons. The stage team was rolling along at probably eight miles an hour.

As the afternoon wore on, we came to the foot of a fairly long hill, known as the 20 Mile House Hill. There was a roadhouse at the bottom of the hill and Mac told me that in the winter months the freight teamsters changed their loads from wagons onto sleighs, as from 20 Mile House on, there was always snow and good sleighing. From the 20 Mile down to Ashcroft there was not enough snow to run a sleigh, the ground being frozen hard and always icy.

I also found out that there had never been any rattlesnakes north of the 20 Mile. Once you leave a sage brush country and lava rock formations you get out of rattlesnake country.

As our team climbed the 20 Mile hill, I could see we had swung away from the Bonaparte River and were heading into another valley which grew a little wider as we progressed. We reached a fine looking ranch, with a log barn and well-cultivated fields, and Mac told me that the ranch was owned by the Dougherty family. It was known as the 23 Mile House. We stayed there overnight and I became acquainted with the head of the family, Charlie Dougherty, a powerfully built young man, a great horseman and a good rancher. In after years I came to know him real well.

The next morning we started on our way again, along a fairly even grade road, passing by several lakes en route. We met several more freight teams and a few riders on saddle horses, most of whom were Indians.

About two o'clock that afternoon we passed by a fair-sized lake, which Mac told me was called Salts Lake, because it had a very high percentage of epsom salts in it. A mile or so further on we came down a sloping hill and the little village of Clinton came into sight. Little did I know at that time, so long ago, that Clinton would be my trading town and headquarters for most all the business I would do in my career.

In those early years Clinton had a real good hotel and a large log barn across the street from the hotel with accommodation for eighty horses. The hotel was the oldest hotel in the Province of British Columbia and was owned by a fine old family named Smith. There was also a large general store, a post office, some provincial government buildings and a blacksmith shop that was doing a roaring trade shoeing freight horses, because no horse would travel the Great Road very long without being shod, as the gravel and rocks soon would make a barefooted horse go lame and tender footed.

Mac and I did not stay very long in Clinton on this my first occasion, as Mac had his orders to stay at the Pollard Ranch, some two miles up The Road from Clinton, located at the foot of the famous Clinton Hill which was over four miles long.

We arrived at this large and well-located Pollard Ranch, which to this day remains in the family. I believe the original John Pollard was a Cornishman who forgot about gold mining and settled on that ranch in 1864. He certainly picked a splendid location. All down the years, the whole area has respected and liked this pioneer family and their descendants. We stayed overnight at the Pollard Ranch. There were three sons and three daughters, all children of the old pioneer Pollard. Their elderly mother lived with them also. We spent a very enjoyable evening there and the next morning we proceeded on our way up The Road. It was not long before we started to climb up a long steep hill, which by necessity of a heavy load, meant lots of stopping to give those good pulling horses a breather. The country on both sides of the hill seemed a lot greener and fresher and The Road was flanked on each side by yellow pine trees, or bull pines as they are often called. There were clouds gathering in the northwestern sky, and it looked to me that we were going to have rain.

We reached the top of Clinton Hill, and The Road levelled out again and a new species of timber appeared on the sides of The Road — a species known as jack-pine. Jack-pine has always been a very much maligned type of timber. While jack-pine has never occupied a front line post in the timber hierarchy it has, and always will have, a most useful part in the construction of log cabins, corrals and rail fences, and as a fuel jack-pine, cut and split, has no competitors as far as quick hot fires and general warmth go.

I noticed rocks after rocks scattered through the jack-pine timber, which set me to wondering if at some time in the early world history there might have been a volcano or earthquake forces in action in this area. However, not being a geologist of any degree, I could not form any authoritative opinion on this matter.

Along towards late afternoon we came to a creek crossing The Road, named the 57 Mile Creek. Two hundred yards beyond we turned to our left in a westerly direction and left the Cariboo Road still pushing its relentless way to the points further north in the great Cariboo. The Cariboo Road was always referred to as "The Road" by all and sundry in those years. The progress and prosperity of a large part of the Cariboo depended, at that time, on how much travel, freight hauling, beef drives and general business surged up and down that famous arterial road.

Before the arrival of the Canadian Pacific Railroad, the old Cariboo Trail started at the little town of Lillooet on the Fraser and the mileage was all taken from Lillooet, hence Clinton was the 47 Mile, The Chasm was the 59 Mile House, the 70 Mile House, the 83 Mile House and on up The Road. However, the arrival of the C.P.R. changed the Cariboo Road starting point to Ashcroft.

After leaving The Road, it became very noticeable to me that the road we were driving along was a lot different from the famous Road we had turned west from. It was quite rough in spots and rocky. There were soft rutted tracks in places where the soil appeared to be alkali. There are two classes of alkali soil, black alkali and white alkali; neither kind is productive of anything but a short sour grass which is unpalatable to any class of livestock.

About a mile after we turned off The Road, heading west, we came to a ranch with log houses and barn, built on a very rocky knob of ground, flanked by a wild hay meadow through which the 57 Mile Creek passed on its way to empty into the Bonaparte River. This place was owned by an old-timer named Jim Bishop who with his wife, two sons and three daughters lived there. They made a good living, running some cattle on the government range in the summer. This 57 Mile used to be a stopping place for all travellers going to and from the Gang Ranch, Dog Creek and the Chilcotin areas, which all lay to the west and northwest of the 57 Mile Ranch.

Mac and I stayed overnight at the Bishop's and I became acquainted with a very good family. In after years I got to know them real well, and appreciated the warm welcome that I always received when at their house.

The next morning we said goodbye to the Bishops and the wheels started rolling on towards the Gang Ranch. Our road threaded its way, more or less, through a parklike country with some open meadows and lakes dotted here and there.

I noticed quite a lot of white-faced Hereford cattle and what looked to me to be a hybrid cross between Hereford and Shorthorn cattle — many of them were straight Hereford, but there were roans and brockle-faced cattle also, which suggested the Hereford-Shorthorn cross to me. They were slick and shining and had lost their old hair from the winter's coat and were starting to put on fat.

In the late afternoon, we came to a log fence running below the road. In due time we came to a ranch situated at the east end of a long lake, called Meadow Lake, which is at least four miles long. This was a typical ranch, with every building made of jack-pine logs, corrals and fences also.

The ranch belonged to a French-Canadian family named Pidgeon. The head of the family, Joe Pidgeon, was a colourful old-timer, who spoke very broken English, well mixed with French and Chinook Indian words. Old Joe was a real hardy gentleman, and on occasion he was tougher than a boiled owl. He had two sons, one of whom was living at Meadow Lake with his wife and two children.

In after years I had many associations with this old-timer and his descendants. The Pidgeons at that time were running over three hundred head of range cattle, and each year cut many tons of a fine quality of wild hay, known as sugar-cane hay.

We started out again next morning, real early. Mac told me that this was a long day ahead of us, as it was twenty-four miles to the Canoe Creek Ranch, where he had orders to stay overnight. After driving along for about four miles, through jack-pine timber on the north side of Meadow Lake, we came out into a stretch of open country with good grass and water and some patches of green poplar trees. Scattered along this open hillside were at least three hundred head of cattle, grazing in this eight- to ten-mile strip of open range.

Below the road all the way ran two lakes, one called White Lake, and the other Long Lake. The water in these two lakes was not good for human drinking, as it was quite alkali, but it looked like there was a spring up on the hill which would be more attractive for the cattle to drink. No livestock care much for alkali water.

Towards noon we came to a long wild hay meadow fenced with a rail fence. There were several log cabins, a barn and a corral. Mac told me that the meadow belonged to the Canoe Creek Indian Reserve and was called Indian Meadows.

It had been raining for two to three hours and the road seemed to be getting a lot softer. The heavy freight wagon wheels cut down in the mud for two or three inches, but we kept on and I could feel the dampness in my underwear, however, there was nothing we could do about it.

The road wound its way down a long hill and at the bottom of the hill there was a log cabin, a barn and a large corral and a small wild hay meadow. This little camp was owned by an old Canoe Creek Indian called Crazy Johnny. We crossed Canoe Creek there and proceeded down a long narrow valley. The Canoe Creek was running below the road and on the upper side of the road there were some high bluffs of limestone rock. I noticed some eagles flying around and figured they had nests high up in the rock bluffs overlooking the road.

In late afternoon we came to the foot of a short but steep little hill and I saw what looked to be a mudhole, probably ten feet long and five feet wide — it was no doubt caused by rain running down the hill with no chance of any outlet to drain. It looked bad and was bad because the hind wheels of our heavy loaded wagon just dropped down over a foot or so and despite all the efforts those fine horses made, we were stuck solid.

Mac said he guessed we'd have to go to Canoe Creek Ranch, which he said was about four miles away, so we unhooked the team. I jumped on old Farmer bareback and Mac jumped on the bay mare, Queen, and we led the other two and finally got to Canoe Creek Ranch house tired, wet and hungry.

There was a lady housekeeper at the ranch named Mrs. Vedum who gave us a real good supper, and the ranch manager, Mr. L. C.

Hammon, who came to British Columbia from away down in Texas, told us that he would lend us some rope and a double block next morning.

Around six-thirty next morning Mac and I went back up the road to pull out the bogged-down freight wagon. By the use of a tree and the double block and good stout rope and the four horses, we managed to pull the loaded wagon out of the hole.

We drove along the road again to the Canoe Creek house. A mile or so this side of the ranch house we passed through the Canoe Creek Indian Reserve in which the cabins and barns were all made of logs. A lot of them seemed to be in very poor shape, but they had a white painted church with a cross gleaming on the top of it and a large bell hanging in a bell tower on top of the church.

In after years I got to know these Indians well, as I had to work with them and was foreman on this Canoe Creek Ranch for over three years. However, I will return to this period later in my story.

Mac and I had to stay overnight again at Canoe Creek Ranch, owing to the delay in being stuck in the bog hole, but next morning started us on our way for the last lap to the Gang Ranch, which Mac said was sixteen miles away.

It was a fine clear day and a gentle breeze, as we wheeled along the road to the Gang. After about four miles the whole country opened up into the valley of the Fraser River, with bunch-grass hills on either side and the road in general following along up the river. The road wound in and out of quite a number of gulches and there were many sharp turns, particularly when driving a four-horse team, because you had to keep your lead team crowded right into the inside bank, on one of those hairpin turns, or else the hind wheels of your wagon would be off the road grade, and that sure meant trouble.

Mac got into a bad jackpot on one of these turns, and the left hind wheel of the wagon was crumbling the edge of the road, with at least a hundred feet or more of straight drop off below us.

I hollered to Mac, "For God's sake, crowd that lead team in to the bank." We were due to roll over the bank and Mac proceeded to get rattled and lose his temper at the horses, snapping his four-horse whip at the lead team, Queen and Maude, but being no good with a four-horse whip, he snapped the whiplash around the heads of the team on the wagon tongue, old Farmer and Dan. Of course it was only a minute or so till all the four horses were so rattled by Mac jerking at their mouths and hitting them on their heads with this whiplash, that the whole outfit refused to pull together.

I was raised in a stock-raising atmosphere, it was in my veins and make-up to know and understand livestock, and seeing those horses so rottenly abused, I couldn't stand it any longer.

"Mac," I said, "give me those lines for a few minutes, I'll get this outfit going up out of this gulch."

"What in hell do you know about handling horses?" he sneered. Of course this snapped the ginger out of me.

"Mac," I told him, "I've forgotten more about handling horses than you'll ever know, and I'll bet you that I can ride or drive horses where you'd be scared to walk afoot."

I took the lines and tied them on the brake rod, and got down and talked in a good gentle smooth way to those horses, giving them an odd pat on their necks. They were all sweating quite a bit and old Farmer in particular was just bug-eyed with fright at being jerked around and snapped over the head with the whiplash. Anyway, I calmed them all down and climbed up on the wagon seat and took the four lines, all even and snug in my fingers, and spoke to the horses — Farmer, Maude and Queen. They all started pulling at once, old Dan doing his best with Farmer, and the wagon inched forward up this short pitch in the gulch. I stopped them a few yards up the pitch and started again and that trouble was over.

I handed the lines back to Mac. "This is your job," I said, "not mine." I don't think Mac liked me any too well for butting in on him. However, he was sure no good with horses in a tight pinch, whether he liked it or not.

It was getting quite late when we turned down a long hill leading to the river and the Churn Creek Ferry, as it was known then. We camped overnight with a government road crew who were getting out timbers from the mountain to install what is now known as the Gang Ranch bridge across the Fraser, which was completed in the late fall of 1912.

In the morning we drove onto the ferry, which at that time was operated by an old Missourian, named Bill Wright, who was quite a character. He had been running the Churn Creek Ferry for quite a few years.

Chapter 2

Starting Work on the Gang Ranch

I GOT OFF THE WAGON at the ferry and being rather dry and hot, as the early morning sun was beating right down on us from a clear blue sky, I dipped my face in that muddy brown Fraser and drank my fill — sand, silt and all. Old Bill looked at me and squirted a bountiful stream of tobacco juice on a big rock alongside the river and said, "Young feller, I guess you must aim to stay in this country quite awhile." I told him I was going to try and stay here for a long time, if I made good.

So Bill said to me, "Anyone drinking this Fraser River water here, will always come back to it again, sooner or later."

I have often thought of his words, how true they were, because somehow or someway, this big old Cariboo acts like a powerful magnet ever drawing the heart, mind and memories of those who have had the experience of living in these big wide open spaces.

The Fraser was very high at this time of the year, as June is a heavy run-off month of snow in the mountains. Trees and old logs were being swept along on that headlong rush to the Pacific Ocean. We crossed the outfit over the river safely and proceeded up a short steep pitch for sixty yards or so and we were on a gentle incline all the way up a long gulch for over two miles.

At the top of a bunch-grass slope the road turned down the sloping hill. What a panorama of size and beauty met my gaze! I saw green hay fields, at least six hundred acres of them, and a cluster of buildings sitting in amidst some native poplar and tall straight Lombardy poplar trees.

This was the Gang Ranch, the finest sight any ranch man would ever like to see, and my home and headquarters, my meal ticket for the next three and a half years, in which time I had many and varied experiences.

It was close to noon on June 7, 1912 when Mac and I arrived at the Gang and Mac drove the big freight wagon alongside a small lumber house, which was the store. In it were supplies of all kinds, from Hudson Bay blankets to plain chewing tobacco. I waited around awhile at the store and along came Mr. Stobie, who had passed us several days earlier, driving a smart trotting pair of bays in a light four-wheeled buggy.

"Well my monny, you made it," were his words when he saw me. I said we'd had a good trip up.

Stobie then told me to bring my blanket roll and showed me a large-sized house that was covered with a light tin sheeting and painted red. He said I'd find a room upstairs and a bed and mattress and maybe I'd have to share the room with one of the other boys, but that made no difference to me.

The dinner bell clanged outside the cook-house, and I made my way over there and sat down at a table with a dozen men — some white men and several half-breeds who were working there.

Stobie himself sat at the head of the long table with us, and I noticed another table on the far side of the dining room, which was fairly well filled with Chinese irrigators and a few Indians. The cook was a Chinaman named Fungo. There was another Chinaman who did all the daily routine chores around there, which were many, and consisted mainly of milking six cows, feeding a bunch of hogs, as the Gang always raised enough pigs to supply the ranch with their own bacon, hams and pork, and the wood for all the stoves was split and carried in from the woodpile by this plodding old Chinese.

I helped unload the big freight wagon after we'd had dinner. I noticed we had hauled up quite a variety of grub — flour, sugar, coffee, tea, beans, rice — mainly essentials of good plain living. I saw a box of butter labelled from New Zealand. Afterwards I found out that although the Gang had over seven thousand head of beef cattle they did not go in for any butter making. What few cows the Chinaman milked, the milk was used in the cook-house and any extras were fed to the fifty-odd head of pigs raised on the ranch each year.

Cowboys and cattlemen have always shied away from cow milking, for some reason or another. It seemed to me that somewhere along the line it hurt their dignity somehow, as they regarded cow milking as one of the lowest down jobs that a human being could fall heir to doing.

Cowboys and Indians would, and could, do 'most anything with cattle, drive them, rope them, brand and castrate them, and many other jobs necessary to the cow business, but to ask them to milk cows, "No Sir." It was taboo to them. Over my years I have known and worked with many good cowhands and cattlemen and have also met a good many who would do no other class of ranch work, except riding a saddle horse and, I'll say this, most of them were real men at their game.

My room mate in the bunkhouse at the Gang was a man named Jim Ragan who had lived in California most of his life, which was around forty years, and he and I became great pals. Jim was a man of many parts, stage driver, bar-tender and a top hand around cattle and horses.

My first morning at the Gang, right after breakfast, Mr. Stobie addressing me by my Christian name said, "Aye now Harry," — the r's in Harry just rolling out like thick Scotch porridge — "and do you know anything about breaking horses mon?" To which I replied that maybe I didn't know it all by any means, but I sure wasn't any greenhorn either, with the result I was told to go help

Jim Ragan break in some eight head of work horse colts that were tied up in the barn. The Gang horse barn had three separate divisions all under the one roof, one side for saddle horses, the centre stable for broke work horse teams and the one Jim and I used was for work horse colts.

We started in to get these colts used to being handled and harness put on them, and to get down to the business of being hooked up. These colts had good stout harness. We'd take the colts out, one at a time, and tie the colt to a blaze-faced old gentle horse called King, and old King really knew his business in educating these unbroke horses. We'd work out two colts in the morning and two more in the afternoon — King being on faithful duty all day long. We'd hook those colts up with old King, on a light strong wagon with a good brake on it. Jim would drive and I'd hold a triprope running down from the hames on the colt's harness down to his front leg and tied to a strap around below his ankle joint. In case the colt got to trying to run away, a quick jerk of the triprope would almost stand the colt on his head. Sometimes some of the colts would get kind of rambunctious, but between Jim and I and faithful old King, we didn't have too much trouble to get them going. After a week or ten days' workout every day, they soon got accustomed to their harness and the rattle of wagon wheels and human handling.

Like everything else in life, a great deal depends on the start-off, and handling unbroke or half broke horses depends on the man who is doing the job. It is no job for a hot-tempered or rattleheaded man, because it calls for patience and firmness, and caution that the colts don't learn bad habits.

The haying season at the Gang was about ready to begin. All the hay fields were seeded down to a mixture of alfalfa and brome grass hay, which made first-class cow feed. Two crops were cut each year, and there would still be another good growth after that, which made for good fall pasture.

After the rough had been taken off these work horse colts, I was told to drive one of them, with another gentle horse, on a hay wagon and get ready to start hauling hay into the stack yards. There were four teams, and sometimes six teams, hauling hay into the stacks, where the load was unloaded by a boom and a mast system and a large two-pronged harpoon fork. The hay load was built in four sections and usually the whole load was unloaded in four big fork loads.

Today the entire system is changed, and almost all ranchers have mechanized equipment. Work horses are a thing of the past on most ranches today. The farm tractor and its many accessories, and its varied usefulness, has now rendered the old horse methods very obsolete. While the tractor and equipment have produced much better and quicker results, it has also produced a very big capital investment wrapped up in a lot of expensive equipment, and requiring a certain amount of technical knowledge to keep this gas and oil run machinery going.

The Gang Ranch is, by far and large, the biggest ranch operation north of the Canadian Pacific Railway in Canada, and ranks second only to the Douglas Lake Cattle Co., which operates south of Kamloops in the Nicola Country of our British Columbia. The Gang Ranch itself and the Gang Range had a natural fence of the Fraser River on the east side and the wild rugged valley of Churn Creek on the south side. Their operations extended as far as Riske Creek in Chilcotin on their northern boundary. They have miles and miles of winter range along the Fraser and Chilcotin Rivers. One year with another most of their cattle, except the calves, bulls and thin cows, all rustled out in these ranges for most of, if not all, the winter. In the spring and summer months, their cattle ranged over a mountain area with bunch-grass openings and scattered timber for about a distance of sixty miles long and around thirty miles wide. I believe they have over sixty thousand acres of deeded, titled land, with a considerable area of leased lands from the Provincial Government of British Columbia.

The basic foundation of the Gang Ranch was outlined by two Virginian brothers, named John and Jerome Harper, who drifted west from Virginia after the Civil War in the 1860's. These two resourceful "boys" were undoubtedly far-sighted and long-headed cattlemen, because they certainly did pick the right locations for running herds of cattle. It was somewhere around 1890 that their holdings were purchased by an English family who built up and consolidated the Gang Ranch and its holdings into the present size of the operation today.

The Gang Ranch got its name from the fact that it was the first ranch in the interior ever to try out a double-furrowed gang plough and so it got a name known as the Gang Ranch, but the Gang had an official name, the Western Canadian Ranching Company Limited, and in 1912 the affairs of the ranch were administered by the grandsons of the old English patriarch — their names were Holland and Prentice, who had homes in Victoria and were also connected with an enterprise known as the B.C. Land and Investment Company of Victoria, B.C.

I could not express, too, what a high degree of respect and liking I had for this fine old English family, the principals of the Company. I always found them to be real fine folks and they were well known all through the Cariboo for their never-failing integrity and human decency. They played a prominent part in all matters of progress in our interior country.

I was, and still am, very proud to know and to remember that I was a trusted employee of theirs and on many occasions I was invited by the famous Bill Holland to enjoy the hospitality and great friendly atmosphere which always prevailed at the Big Tyee House, as their own private home at the Gang was called.

The entire holdings of the Gang Ranch were sold out to two American millionaires from Montana and Idaho, U.S.A., and the whole interior of our Southern Cariboo watched the passing of this fine Old Country family, with a silent sorrow at their leaving.

I hauled hay at the main Gang Ranch during all the haying season of 1912 and it was away in the middle of November when the last of it was stacked. I would think that there were about forty-five of us in the haying crew. At the close of haying, the Chinese irrigators all left and most of them wintered in Ashcroft.

The late fall arrived and the Gang got down to a fall and winter crew of about a dozen of us. I and another fellow were detailed off to haul firewood logs on a wagon for the next year's wood supply. It took many days for two of us to haul those logs down to the main buildings.

One day when I was driving my team and wagon en route for more logs I ran across an old white-haired man who was driving an old white horse in a two-wheeled cart. He spoke with a very deep voice which rumbled out of his long matted beard. The old man looked at me and said, "Stranger, that God damned gate of Stobie's fell down on me as I went to shut it and I had to lift on the gate so hard, that the piles were sticking out of my rear end that far,

Stranger." And he made an expressive move along his hand, to let me know how far his piles had protruded.

I told the old man that I was sorry I wasn't there in time to help him with the gate, and the old boy proceeded to dig and scratch violently under his armpits.

"The gol-darned exemia has got a real holt on me, Stranger," he said. However, he drove on down the rough road to the Gang buildings and I saw him again at supper time.

This old character's name was Wycott. Everyone called him "Stranger Wycott" largely because to everyone he always started off with "Stranger . . ." Stranger Wycott was a very early old-timer and although very old, his mind was clear and he told me of his arrival in British Columbia from California around 1859—how he had thirty head of pack horses, known as a pack train, and he used to load his pack horses each with a two hundred pound pack, and pack from Lillooet to Barkerville for eight cents a pound. Stranger Wycott used to winter his pack horses along the north side of Churn Creek. He also had some cattle ranging in there. He was old and the cattle and horses all eventually got wild and really running wild stock. I saw twelve- to fifteen-year-old bulls with big wide horns and not a brand on them, none of them castrated either. After Wycott's death in 1914 the Gang Company bought all his cattle and horses on that Churn Creek range. It sure did take a lot of courage, ability and know-how to get those cattle rounded up.

I was telling Jack MacIntyre who was in charge of all the cattle on the Gang, under Andy Stobie's orders, how I had encountered old Stranger and how the old man had complained of this exemia bothering him, and Mac just smiled and said, "Old Stranger was always lousier than hell, that's what made him scratch."

Jack MacIntyre was a very quiet slow-speaking man, and he sure did know the cow business from one end to the other. He used to have three or four Indian boys riding with him and in the winter months, good weather and bad, Mac and the boys were riding the winter ranges, keeping track of the cattle, bringing in any cows that needed to be fed hay.

Andy Stobie, with whom by this time I had become on very friendly terms, detailed me and a fellow called Gillis off to feed five hundred and fifty calves, which took four good big loads of alfalfa every day.

Christmas 1912 arrived and we had a big feed of turkeys and Christmas puddings and a considerable supply of rum which all added to the joyful feelings and the good fellowship of this yearly occasion. Christmas Day was always quite an important ranch institution in those early years.

Around the first week in February 1913, Stobie came to me and told me he wanted me and two other boys to go and camp up on a mountain about twelve miles above the Gang, in the timber, and for us to cut at least eight hundred saw logs and to skid them up into a big log pile, for sawing into lumber for the ranch when the spring arrived. We proceeded to a cabin on a small creek in the timber and, with crosscut-saw and axes and my team for skidding the logs out with grub, blankets, hay and oats, etc., we made a camp for the balance of the winter.

I had two good boys with me at that camp, one named Denis Pidgeon from Trois Rivières in old Quebec, and the other one named Barney Page who had drifted in from the States. Denis Pidgeon was a nephew of the famous old Joe Pidgeon of Meadow Lake, and like nearly all French Canadians I have ever known and worked with, he was a natural born axe man and a good partner on the end of a crosscut-saw.

Barney did the cooking, and limbed up trees in his spare time. The grub, of course, was of the very plain but substantial style with lots of mulligan stews of beef, carrots and onions; with coffee and baking powder bannocks and stewed prunes for a dessert to top off our dinner and supper meals. Barney prided himself on his cooking abilities, and one day he confided to me that when he was cooking for a fair-sized bunch and there were any complaints on his cooking efforts, he used to leave the soapy dish-water just dry on the dishes and give the boys the back door trots, which cancelled out the complaints. However, I told him I wouldn't be kicking on his cooking as long as the grub was cooked. I could eat 'most anything, and Barney certainly knew how to turn out a good bunch of hotcakes, which were always the big end of our daily breakfasts.

I had to make several trips through the deep snow to the Gang for more hay, grain and grub during the winter and Mr. Stobie came up once to see how things were going. Around the middle of March, we had over eight hundred logs from twelve to sixteen feet long, all cut and piled up, eight to ten logs high on the skidway, ready for the spring saw milling.

We all returned to the ranch about the 20th of March and I was given the job of hauling hay, and hauling out some dead cattle from the feed grounds to the edge of a steep hill above Gaspard Creek, which ran into the Fraser. I rolled the dead carcasses off the steep bank down on to the creek bottom, and by the look of that pile of bones, I figured that there must have been many dead cattle at one time or another. Of course any cow outfit the size of the Gang Ranch could not escape having some deaths and casualties in such a big operation.

It was on the 29th of March, 1913, that a little short coupled-up man, with a wide ten-gallon Stetson hat on, riding boots and a black silk handkerchief around his throat, came riding into the ranch around supper time. He had ridden up the river from an outlying pasture about thirty-three miles south of the Gang, called the "Crow's Bar Pasture," which belonged to the Gang Ranch and is still owned by them.

His name was Mike O'Brian and he was of the typical cowboy type who ranged all the way from Texas and California to the British Columbia and Alberta cow country.

Chapter 3

I Take Over the Crow's Bar

AFTER SUPPER that evening I was out in the barn at the Gang, giving my team their grain and brushing them off for the night, when Mr. Stobie came into the barn, looked around and said, "Aye mon, Har-r-r-r-r-ry I want to see you Mon." So without any further comment I followed him up to his office, which was next to his bedroom in the main Gang Ranch house and cook-house.

Stobie asked me if I would like to ride down the river and take over the management of this Crow's Bar pasture, as Mike O'Brian was quitting and someone had to be sent to replace him. He told me my job would be to look after five hundred head of steers and spayed heifers. I had a cabin to stay in and I'd have to batch, which meant do my own cooking. I'd have to be responsible for these cattle, so after some meditation on the matter, I decided I'd take the job and be the representative man for the Gang Ranch at their Crow's Bar operation.

The next morning after breakfast, I threw my saddle on a big bay horse named Whisper and Mike and I started down the river to the Crow's Bar Pasture. We rode along the wagon road till we reached Canoe Creek and then turned down the river on a long trail through gulches, flats, and sidehills on the Canoe Creek Ranch's winter range, and after around twelve miles, the trail left the river and pushed its way upward through some more open flats and fir timber, till about five o'clock that evening we came to a gate and a barbed wire fence which Mike told me was part of the Crow's Bar Pasture. About a mile or so further along the trail, we came to a log cabin, built close to the edge of a low-lying gulch. This cabin, Mike told me, was the Crow's Bar cabin, and until I left there for overseas service at the end of December 1915, this cabin was my home.

After we'd had a bite of breakfast next morning, Mike pulled out, riding a small roan gelding which was his own saddle horse. He was a silent, non-committal sort of a fellow and I figured he was maybe sick, or not feeling good, as he did not offer to tell me anything about the job — what to do or what needed doing most. However, I thought I'd soon see for myself what needed to be done. I didn't see Mike again for quite a while and when I did see him, he was driving the Clinton to Dog Creek and Alkali Lake mail stage, making a weekly run between these points, carrying the mail and any odd passengers and small freight items.

However, I started to look around and size up the situation and it came upon me, that as I was in charge of the outfit, I'd really try to make good. I felt that Stobie at the Gang certainly trusted me, and I was in a spot where for the first time in my life I had to make my own decisions, and to figure and plan out and lay out my work, and attend to the most important things first.

There was a rickety old barn down in the gulch from the cabin and little or no hay in it, and there was a real good spring a few yards from the cabin, and about three hundred yards away there was a little pile of rye hay in an old stack yard. There were no signs of any place I could pasture my saddle horse close, without having to picket him or hobble him. The rye hay was all bleached out, just like straw, so the second night I picketed my horse, with my lasso rope, tying one end of the rope just below his ankle and the other end I tied to a small dead cottonwood limb, just heavy enough for my horse to pull a little bit and I felt sure he could not drag it too far by morning. It is always a poor thing to do, to picket a horse and tie the rope to something that is real solid, because he could pull his shoulder out if he got scared and started to run.

I had two saddle horses, the one I rode down from the Gang and the other one was a pinto-coloured gelding. He had a real pinto eye and I called him Pinto and he turned out to be a real good cow horse, and tougher than a boiled owl. He sure could stand lots of hard riding. There was a team of black work horses and they were just right for any little old jobs that I needed them for. They would run away at the drop of a hat, but I never had any trouble with them.

With Mike gone, I started to ride around this big Crow's Bar pasture and see what I had come down to look after. It looked to me that Crow's Bar had two distinct divisions of the large area; there was a mountain part and a river winter range part. In the winter months the cattle ranged down along the river, the strip of winter range being about five miles long, and in the spring and summer months these beef heifers and steers were turned out on the government range, then rounded up most generally in the early November of each year.

I had some grub in the cabin, which I knew would last me for maybe a month or so. Every day for the first two weeks or so, I'd ride down on the winter range, sizing up the cattle and the grass and finding out the location of the several springs where the majority of the cattle watered every day. Night-time found me back up on the mountain at the cabin and I'd water my horse, and picket him by the front foot to the light dry pole. Then I'd head into the cabin and cook my supper. Some nights the supper was a little bit rough, but I had plenty of hot baking powder biscuits, fried salt pork and some beans or rice and most always I had stewed prunes for dessert. I always liked prunes, they were good for the old stomach and kept a fellow in good order which is a very satisfactory daily event of good living.

I noticed before I had been very many days at the cabin that I had several fair-sized grey birds every morning, hopping and flying around the cabin door, looking for any scrap that I threw outside from the table. They were whiskey-jacks or camp robbers and they grew quite tame as soon as they found I wasn't going to hurt them.

I had other visitors every so often in the shape of long sharp-faced, long-tailed rats which were known as pack rats. These varmints would pack chips, knives and anything they could drag along from one end of the cabin to the other, always at night-time. They were sure a destructive pest and I found an old rusty trap in the old barn and I cleaned it up and sometimes I'd get one in the trap. Sometimes at night when they would wake me up I'd light my coal oil lamp and keep real quiet and I'd shoot one with my gun once in a while. I have always hated pack rats; sometimes you get a variety of human pack rat who'd steal the holes out of a tin whistle if there was no one around.

The winter range in old Crow's Bar was almost all open country with more or less gentle slopes of bunch-grass hills and flats along the river, although the trail down from the mountain was fairly steep in places, the cattle were all strong and in good shape, being mostly coming two-year-olds and coming three-year-old spayed heifers and a small sprinkling of steers. It was a real pretty sight to see those cattle strung out for several miles, feeding on the flats or lying down in various bedding grounds. Spring was well along and I saw numbers of deer feeding on the young green grass on the sidehills.

Each spring, during those years, the Gang used to take a certain quota of their heifer calves, generally around 230 head, and drive them down the river to Crow's Bar. It took three days to drive them and after my first year there I would ride up to the Gang around the middle of March and I and two more cowhands would bring them down. Around early May, before the real hot weather came and the flies, these heifers were introduced to the operation of spaying, which simply amounted to de-sexing them. The process of spaying these heifers was an operation in which it was most important to know exactly what you were doing, otherwise you would be in real trouble and maybe lose some.

Stobie, my boss, and Jack MacIntyre, and about five other cowboys would ride down from the Gang and I would have the heifer calves all rounded up and in the big corral about a half mile below the cabin the night before — the reason being that these heifers were better to be hungry than full of grass as it was then easier to spay them. The calves were roped by the hind feet, thrown down and stretched out between wooden posts and their hair clipped down low on their left side. Stobie would then make an incision in their left side and with sleeves rolled up would gently push his left hand inside the heifer, cut loose from the calf web, their two ovaries. This was done with a long ebony-handled knife, known as a spaying knife. The heifer was then stitched up with three cross stitches, drawing the incision pretty close together. A healing ointment and some lard were mixed and spread over the wound and it was then smeared over with pine tar for the purpose of keeping out the flies.

The de-sexing of these heifer calves made quite a change in their behaviour and way of life. It certainly set them back physically for a couple of months, but after that they picked up considerably and became real good beef critters with a tough wiry stamina, and hardy. If they ever became really excited they were rough, tough customers to handle at times and they made real good beef—sometimes, if anything, they got too fat.

The practice of spaying heifers has now been almost wiped out in the cow business and the large ranches worked out a principle that any heifer reaching the age of three and not having a calf that summer would automatically be shipped for beef that fall, as in the cow business the female is regarded first and last as a machine for producing calves and no cattleman can afford to keep cows and feed them for two winters on just one calf, so if the average cow does not have a calf in the spring or early summer she is shipped to the packing plant usually in the early fall.

I was always glad to see this annual spaying job completed as I had to cook for all the hands while they were there, which meant quite a lot of extra work for me, because I still had to take my place on the job. When they headed their horses up the trail back to the Gang I was sure glad to see them go. Cooking for one or two is not too bad, but cooking for a bunch is entirely different unless you have plenty of time to do it — rice, beans and spuds are very important articles when cooking for a bunch of hungry cowboys.

About two weeks after the cowboys had all left from the spaying trip I saw that I'd have to go and get myself a load of grub so I caught the team that was running out in the big bunch-grass flat a little ways from the cabin and I got up real early and hooked up the team to a wagon I had there and started out for the Gang. This was a forty-five mile trip and I got there just in time for supper.

Two mornings later I started back for Crow's Bar with the wagon loaded with enough grub to do me for five or six months but it took me two days to get back with the loaded wagon. However, I had lots of good plain grub with the good old salt pork, rice and beans, flour, sugar and coffee, and the ever-faithful prunes for the finishing off titbit of the daily diet. I used very little butter, mostly lard and pork fat to smear over the hot biscuits, and corn syrup for my hotcakes.

The cabin I had at Crow's Bar was a good comfortable log cabin, but I found out one day that it did not have nearly enough dirt on the poles which were laid across the roof on the ridge logs. It started to rain and for three days and nights it poured down rain and pretty soon the roof started to leak like a sieve, and towards the end of the third day I had just one spot in the cabin that did not leak. When it finally quit raining I got up on the roof and shovelled off the few inches of wet dirt and started in to fix the roof right. I dug into some old rye hay I had around the old barn and hauled it over to the cabin and I threw about ten inches of it on the roof. The old rye hay on the poles prevented the dirt from sifting down on to the floor of the cabin and with ten inches of dirt on the roof I had a leak-proof one, warm in the winter and cool in the summer. It lasted for many years.

This job finished, I started to turn the cattle out on the government range. There was some real good bunch-grass slopes to the north side of the Crow's Bar pasture and there was surely some fine grass in the close-in areas. It was good range and stayed that way till the arrival of the homesteaders a year or so later.

I had not been very long at Crow's Bar before I discovered that there were some neighbour ranchers in that area to the south of Crow's Bar down in the creek bottom of Big Bar Creek. This long narrow valley was sprinkled with settlers living on the creek, most of them with just more or less a good garden patch, with the exception of two very old pioneer families, the Grinders and the Kosterings who had real good places on the banks of the Fraser, at the mouth of Big Bar Creek, and they irrigated their fields from Big Bar Creek and raised a lot of good crops, mostly alfalfa hay, fruit and vegetables of all kinds. In fact, anything could be grown along that Fraser River as long as it had water and heat.

At this time in 1913, the head of the Grinder family was a slightly-built little man called Phil. This kindly old chap was a Pennsylvanian Dutch by birth. He had come up the Fraser looking for gold in the early 1860's and had decided to settle at Big Bar. Of course, in due time he got himself an Indian lady who was the daughter of the Chief of a tribe of Indians living down the river from Big Bar. Nancy was her name, and old Phil and Nancy lived together for many years on that ranch and raised half a dozen children and were respected and liked by all.

Old Phil had a great sense of humour and loved to get a practical joke on anyone he could, and I had many an interesting talk with him and laughed my head off at some of his practical jokes and his ever ready wit. One time I was talking to old Phil and remarked that the mountains across the river looked pretty steep to me, and Phil advised me very strongly and said, "Harry, if you are ever riding your saddle horse coming down those trails off those mountains, be sure and keep your shirt collar all snugged up around your neck because riding down hill is so steep that a horse might drop a hot bun right down your neck." And I always remembered his advice.

Twice a year Phil would make a pilgrimage to Clinton with the team and wagon for grub, and each trip the old gentleman would stay three or four days visiting around and drinking rum with his old cronies, if any of them happened to be around.

One evening Phil was getting into his bed, in the large big room in the old Clinton Hotel, the room being full of single spring beds, and generally well occupied by freighters, cowboys and outside travellers, all sleeping in this one big room. He noticed that the occupant of the next bed to his was a very dignified and reserved Englishman, with riding britches and hunting boots and a real nice coat, evidently some Britisher who was looking over the Cariboo, probably for ranching purposes. Phil had been bending his elbow considerably in the line of beer and rum and during the night he woke up, and looking around he could find no chamber to piddle in so being of a resourceful nature he used the Englishman's riding boot for the utensil. Morning came and the high-class Englishman got up and started to dress, and of course put his foot into his fine hunting boot. He gave a cry of horror and dismay and said, "Oh, someone has been using my blarsted boot as a chamber." To this old Phil drawled, "Well stranger, I looked around to beat hell but I couldn't find anything, so I had to use your boot. I sure hope you ain't got no hard feelings about it." The Britisher gave Phil a very strong look, emptied his boot and pulled it on again, and I'll bet he sure figured he'd come to one hell of a rough country.

In those years the sight of an Old Country Englishman, speaking with a highly polished Oxford English accent, with riding britches and leggings, or hunting boots, was always an opportunity for the deadbeats to take an unfair advantage, for the Britisher had never been trained or brought up in the atmosphere of hot air, bullshit and plain and fancy lying. It often was a very expensive deal for him as most of them were greener than the grass and figured that everyone spoke the truth. Nevertheless, there were many of them who made out real well after they became more or less range broke and more "civilized" and used to the ways of our country.

Chapter 4

Some of the Neighbours

IN AN EASTERLY DIRECTION from the Crow's Bar pasture, across a bunch-grass area of at least three thousand acres, lay the old Haller homestead which was settled around the year 1870.

Old Joe Haller was a Bavarian who emigrated to British Columbia in the early days of the Barkerville gold rush in 1859, and later settled down on Big Bar Creek about fifteen miles from the Fraser River. In later years this place became the O K Ranch, in which, for seventeen years of my active career I had a very prominent part in building, in this big and expansive strip of the Southern Cariboo.

Big Bar Creek, in the years around 1913, was largely settled with relatives and descendants of the three families of white settlers, the Grinders, the Kosterings and the Hallers. They had intermarried considerably and were more or less all related. Times were often quite hard for them but they managed to get along. They all grew a garden and deer were very plentiful. Each year the salmon ran up the Fraser River to their spawning grounds in the Chilco Lake area.

Everyone, Indians and settlers alike, would go down to the river and catch salmon with a net drawn around a light pole. In the fast running water the salmon had to hug the side of the river to keep moving but quite a lot were caught each year. The salmon were salted in a barrel or small keg and sometimes were smoked or hung on poles to dry in the sun.

The folks on the Big Bar Creek were a resourceful bunch. They had little or no cash, but the men had jobs in the summer, either on ranches or government road crews, who at that time made roads and repaired them — the work all being done by shovels and teams of horses, which today are all replaced by big high-powered road machines, and which have accomplished much more than in the old horse days, but at a terrific cost of capital and a heavy upkeep to their operator.

On the north and east boundaries of Crow's Bar were several miles of government range with considerable open grazing, and at this time there were only two men on the mountain, each with a homestead within a mile or so of the Crow's Bar pasture; about eight miles away there lived an Irishman named Tom Derbe who was quite a puzzle to me in many ways.

Derbe kept absolutely to himself and was a very unsociable neighbour. Although many times I did him a good neighbourly turn, I was never invited into his big log house to meet his wife and little daughter. Derbe always met me at the door and gave me a very frigid reception so I soon learned to leave him plumb alone. There is an old saying in the cow business that a man may not have many friends but he sure as hell needs a neighbour and it was too bad that Derbe did not remember that; however, I will tell more of this further on.

I formed a great liking and respect for Billy and Minnie Grinder who, as Phil got older, took over the running of the Grinder Ranch at Big Bar. Billy was married to one of the Kostering girls, and in all my life I have never known a finer couple. They were the last word in hospitality and human kindness, and they always had a place at their table for all and sundry who came along. Not only did they raise and take care of their own family, but they also raised all the homeless children in that Big Bar country. I am not a front rank hymn singer where religion is concerned, but I will take a bet that the good Lord will have a reserved seat for this fine old couple at the last roundup of the world, and I am so glad that now, at the closing years of their lives, they are so comfortable and free from worries.

The summer months passed along quietly and I was busier than a bird dog, fixing fences and making a few improvements to the cabin and barn, and I also built a horse pasture close to the cabin so that I would not have to continue picketing my horse, and things began to shape up like a pretty snug little home.

I rode the range many days each month looking at the Gang Ranch heifers and sizing up their condition and progress. I got so I could pick out those heifers from quite a distance away — they had something about them, different from other cattle on the range. One thing was very noticeable, they were much wilder than most of the others, which were principally cows, calves and yearlings belonging to the Grinders and the Kosterings.

In late October I got two Indians from the Canoe Creek tribe to help me gather and round up the Gang Ranch heifers and steers on the range. The first two weeks we did a real land office business rounding up those fat, slick and well-bred beef heifers and gathered about 425 head out of the 500 the Gang Ranch had turned out. I made a point of counting the cattle when I turned them out and when I gathered them in. The last fifty to seventy-five head were usually scattered sometimes as far as thirty miles away, and it took lots of riding to get them so they would follow and get mixed up with the other cattle. Many times I would pick up cattle that belonged to other ranches over twenty miles away.

There was always a golden, unwritten law in the cow business, amongst good cattlemen, that you would never leave a critter standing in the snow away out somewhere; you would always pick it up and put it in with yours and the first chance you got you sent the owner word that you had one or more of his animals and he would come and get them.

All the cattle running on the government range were branded with the owner's brand — the brand being the proof of ownership — and most of the cattle carried a flesh mark of some description. Some ranchers split one ear, or both, and others cut a small dewlap on the brisket or other parts. These flesh marks helped out a lot in identifying the animal, but the brand always settled legal ownership. Occasionally you might run across a calf without a brand on it. Sometimes the cow would die for some reason or another and the calf would be left without a mother, in which case it grew up an orphan calf or a "slick-ear."

I usually had the cattle well rounded up by the middle of December and after New Year's my boss, Andy Stobie, and Jack MacIntyre and probably four other cowboys, would ride down from the Gang Ranch and round up the three-year-old heifers and the odd four-year-olds and we would start the annual beef drive from the Crow's Bar pasture to the Perry Ranch which was located about seven miles from Ashcroft on the Canadian Pacific main line. It took us about seven days to get the beef drive down there travelling about ten to fifteen miles a day, the cattle making about two miles an hour, and whenever we came to an open patch of range, after driving along for a few miles, we would hold up the herd for a little rest and feed, if there was any grass near the road.

We had some real good cowhands at the Gang Ranch in those years, all good men on a horse with lots of good judgement in handling cattle. One in particular was a boy named Cliff Coldwell, who was raised in Idaho, and at that time Cliff broke all the saddle horses for the Gang, each year breaking around twenty-five head of coming four-year-old colts. Cliff had a wonderful disposition, always joking and humming a little tune as he drove the cattle along, and when he was finished breaking a horse, you could sure make it turn on a nickel and give you some change.

When our beef drive arrived at the Perry Ranch near Ashcroft, which was owned and operated by the Gang Ranch, the beef heifers were put into several large feed yards and given alfalfa hay and grain for a period of two to three months. During that time one or two carloads were shipped each week or two to the coast markets and meat packing plants in Vancouver.

The Perry Ranch was managed by a Scotchman named Bill Murdock, and whenever the beef drive was handed over to him, we all took off for Ashcroft for a day and a night. Of course, all being a little young and foolish we tried to paint the town red, but we always ran out of paint, and the next day we would start back home riding up as far as Clinton the first day, and the next morning we started for home. I went to Crow's Bar, Mac and the others all heading for the Gang Ranch. Most of us broke, but happy.

Those annual beef drives were the only link we had with civilization, however, I did not miss the sound of a locomotive nor the association of people living and working in towns and cities. I would never exchange the life of living in the big wide open spaces of the Cariboo for a life in a town as there was always a big variety of jobs from shoeing saddle horses to building fences and log cabins. And there were the long day rides after cattle, watching the cows munching down the green grass, the little white-faced calves bucking and playing near their ma's — their little bellies full of good warm milk as they sucked and slobbered down their rich succulent diet from their mothers' udders. In my humble honest opinion, there is no life that can compare with living right with old Mother Nature, although I am sure that the financial returns from this sort of life will never compare with the results achieved by the town and city dwellers engaged in business and the pursuit of the almighty dollar in their industrial and professional careers.

Chapter 5

Homesteaders on Big Bar Mountain Range

THE WINTER OF 1913 came to an end and in early March the snow was getting very soft and mushy on the flats and sidehills along the Fraser and on the winter ranges. In due time the sun got stronger and warmer, and deer on the sidehills began to nibble the young green grass as it peeped through the earth, and I began to meditate and plan about my 1914 spring operations — what I had to do in the coming season.

I rode up the river from Crow's Bar to the main Gang, and started back down the trail about three days later with around 230 head of heifer calves. I had two extra men to help me take them down to Crow's Bar — all these heifer calves had to be spayed during the first ten days of May, and in number they replaced the beef drive which had left Crow's Bar in early January.

It took me three long days to drive these heifer calves down that river trail which was about thirty miles in all, and the calves proceeded to range all over the Crow's Bar pasture, just wolfing down all the grass they could find, and there was certainly lots of grass in that Crow's Bar in those years.

The old-timer, Stranger Wycott, went on over the big old High Mountain in the spring of 1914. He died in a little log cabin behind the blacksmith's shop at the Gang Ranch and the old pioneer had nine one-hundred dollar bills sewed up in a little sack which was stitched to his underdrawers. I guess like a good many other old-timers I have known, old Stranger was very cautious and distrustful of having money in a bank.

A few days after Stranger Wycott passed on I was riding down on Big Bar Creek and was going through the Grinder Ranch on my way back up to the mountain and I happened to see old Phil Grinder sitting in his chair with the sunshine warming up his old bones. I stopped my horse and talked to the old gent for a few minutes and happened to mention that his old compadre, Stranger Wycott, had died a few days earlier at the Gang. Old Phil Grinder turned in his chair and said to me, "Harry, ain't a man a damn fool to die in the spring?" And I said, "I guess you're right, Phil, but none of us has too much to say about how long we figured on staying in this old world."

However, old Phil must have had it all figured out because he hung on till late December of that year, 1914, then contracted pneumonia. Of course, at his old age of nearly 96, the rugged old settler was not able to win the battle.

The spring of 1914 saw the arrival of quite a few more settlers and homesteaders in this Crow's Bar and Big Bar Mountain areas. Most of them were from around the Southern Alberta country, and it was only a matter of a few months until the range outside the Crow's Bar pasture was dotted with homesteads, and the new settlers had high hopes of growing some crops and raising some cattle. The arrival of these homesteaders had the effect of pushing the Gang Ranch heifers and the other range cattle further back on the range, to the timbered and rougher sections of the area, and homesteaders' cabins and fences began to show up right outside the Crow's Bar pasture.

I didn't take too kindly to the arrival of these settlers in the Big

Bar Mountain areas, as it seemed to me that barbed wire fences, ploughed ground, homesteaders and their wives and kids, milk cows, chickens and a school, all were the forerunners of trouble and limitations for the cattlemen, as indeed it has always been whenever settlement and a certain amount of civilization invaded the open range areas.

Every rancher and stockman must have a considerable amount of elbow room to be able to extend his operations, and you just can't run cows in any country where you can look out of the kitchen door and see your neighbour's washing hanging on his clothes line because you would wake up and find you didn't have enough grass to last a saddle horse out for one night's feed, and no man can make a success out of owning a hundred and sixty acre homestead as far as a cow ranch goes, unless he can find ways and means to enlarge and build up, from a real small start.

There were about a dozen settlers in all on that Big Bar Mountain range and most of them arrived with just enough grub and tools to make a bit of a start, hoping of course that the good Lord would send plenty of rain and moisture to enable them to make a living growing crops and raising a few head of cattle.

Most of these folks had originally come from the United States and they already had the necessary pioneer toughness, which is so much a part of living in a back beyond situation, as a large amount of toughness was the keynote of survival.

A tough, wiry old gent named "Zim" Zimmerlee drove in there from Oregon State with a four-horse team and a covered wagon, a wife and several children. It had taken old Zim Zimmerlee the best part of two years to finally arrive on that Big Bar Mountain range, but he told me that he could not travel every day en route because his horses would get tired and leg weary and he would have to rest them awhile. In the resting spells they would work a few days here and there to help buy grub. Zim and his missus were a good hard-working couple and I would judge them to belong to the same rugged class of settlers that crossed the plains, fought Indians, Mormons and cattle barons all the way from Missouri to California.

Zim was a tough old snoozer. I know that he cut his knee open with an axe and sewed it up with some worsted yarn and his wife's darning needle. Another time he got one of his front teeth knocked out by a kick in the mouth while branding a calf, and he whittled out a wooden tooth from a soft poplar stick with his jack-knife and jammed it down between his teeth again, and closed the gap. He was nearly sixty-four years young then and I asked him why he bothered to do this to which he replied, "I'll be goddamned if I'll spoil my good looks with a tooth out."

Well, he was a hardy old chap, and it took a very rough jolt to make any dent in the calibre of a man like Zimmerlee. He belonged to that reliable bunch of real old American pioneers, whose spirit and morale were simply unbeatable.

There were several other homesteaders on that Big Bar Mountain range who are well worth a note of remembrance. Charlie Wilson, a South Dakota boy who was trying to make a living raising some horses, a good-hearted fellow who never quit talking, and voicing his opinions, and never got to sell a horse because he would want such a high price for it.

There was Sandy Bandhauer, nicknamed for his shock of real red hair, who by long days of hard work managed to eke out a living for himself, his wife and their three nice young girls. A family named Wilkinson came there from England and started with nothing and built up a home and raised a few cattle and some turkeys every year, but the low rainfall, hot winds, drought and grasshoppers took a very serious toll of their hard and frugal efforts to get ahead.

I was often able to give some of these settlers a few days' work in helping me repair the eighteen miles of barbed wire fence that I was responsible for.

There were two brothers named Al and Andrew Neas who were good capable stockmen from the Cardston country in Southern Alberta. Al was sure a good man with a lasso rope, and I never saw him once that he missed when he was throwing his loop over a horse's head, and any horse that Al ever broke to ride you could figure he'd be well broke, as he certainly was a real horse breaker.

A family called Perkins came in from Oregon, and they did their best to make a ranch, raising quite a few hogs each year, especially if they were lucky enough to raise a little rye or wheat to fatten them on. For a while we had a young fellow named Ernest Thorenson, who homesteaded quite a rock pile, and lasted for about two years or so.

To give these settlers credit, I think they meant well and had the consuming idea to make a home for themselves and their children, but it proved to be a very tough task for them, because while the soil would grow crops, ripen wheat and oats, and grow some hardy vegetables, the lack of rainfall was the big problem. Without the rain at the right time the grain would dry out in the warm breezes that used to sweep over the mountains from the Fraser and Thompson River valleys.

There were possibly only one or two good crops every five years. The going was pretty tough for these folks and in later years the grasshoppers came in and the dry farmers, as they were called, really did come in for a lot of hard times. The hoppers would cut off the heads of the wheat or oats and just leave a bunch of grain stalks sticking up and would change a fairly promising stand of grain into a very miserable and disheartening picture, and while the provincial department made efforts to help them poison the hoppers, no worthwhile stamping out was ever accomplished in those days with the dry summers, eternal hot winds and cloudless skies.

The settlers are all gone from that area today and some have died and their children are scattered in other better places. All in all, the settlement of that Big Bar Mountain range ended in a dismal failure for all concerned. A large area of that range was ploughed up and after years of partial and sometimes total crop failure, it has taken years for the natural grass to return to anything like it was originally.

It is a great mistake to turn a real good cow country into a farming country, especially where the rainfall is so small and unpredictable. The agricultural tyees in both Canada and the United States have taken a wise view in respect to allowing settlement in areas today that are questionable as to sufficient rainfall and moisture. In those days of 1912, and for many years thereafter, if a man figured he could carve out a ranch and a home in a half-dry country, he was given a chance, and the results always showed that he had to give up and move away to a rain belt area, or to some valley or district where irrigation would grow his crops and at least give him some return for his hard efforts.

Chapter 6

Riding Up The Road

ALONG IN EARLY June of 1914 — the annual bunch of scrubby yearling heifers having been all spayed and picking up again after their operations — I rode up the river on my old Pinto and asked my boss, Andy Stobie, if I could get a couple of weeks or so off. I wanted to ride "Up Country" as far as Barkerville which lay about sixty miles in a northeasterly direction from the little town of Quesnel on the far stretches of the Cariboo Road. I wanted to take a look around and see if I could find some more cow country. I'd had a pretty fair run on the grindstone, so I figured a couple of weeks change would be as good as a rest.

Stobie told me that it would be all right for not more than three weeks at the most — and I told him I'd be back under that time. So back down the river I rode, and in the next day or so I started out, with a clean shirt and underwear, a good ten-gallon Stetson and a good black silk handkerchief around my neck, good rigging in the line of a good saddle, bridle, boots and spurs and a real good raw-hide lasso rope, and a good chunk of a saddle horse I called Pilot. I knew he'd carry me thirty-five miles a day without any trouble as long as he had a bite of feed and a drink of water — kind of often and regular.

I rode up the river as far as the Gang on my first day, and of course stayed there overnight, and my old friend, Jack MacIntyre, unlimbered his usual silent tongue to wise me up to the short cuts on the trail to the Chilcotin River. In the morning I stepped up on old Pilot, and headed him over the trail up the river.

The trail spun its way along the higher benches of the river and along about two o'clock in the afternoon I rode on up through a timbered slope and when I reached the top of the ridge I could see a river tearing along from the west. To me it looked like it joined up with the Fraser about four miles east of this ridge and I knew at once that I had come on to the Chilcotin River.

I got off my horse, Pilot, and let him feed for awhile on a little open spot, reached into the gunny sack I had tied behind my saddle and fished out a little bite of lunch that I had talked out of old Fungo — the cook at the Gang — and while I was eating this bread and beef sandwich I was turning my head around just like it was on a swivel and sizing up my bearings.

On the north side of the Chilcotin were at least ten miles of bunch-grass flats and slopes running down to the river — so I knew that they were the Gang Ranch steer range pastures. If I rode on far enough I'd finally get in sight of the company cabin on the Chilcotin — and I felt kind of sure I'd find Jim Ragan there. He was in charge of the Chilcotin range for the Gang.

I caught Pilot and started on the trail up the river, and after riding for about eight miles the trail took a turn down a long ridge and I came to a bridge on the Chilcotin — which I crossed. The river was sure aboiling down through that canyon, just arunning like the mill tails of Hell, and looking at it, I figured a man would never have a Chinaman's chance of ever getting out alive, if he ever got in there.

About a mile and a half up the trail from the bridge, I could see a log cabin and a log barn and a small green patch, and I knew this must be the cabin so I let Pilot take his time climbing up the long hog's back trail. I rode up to the barn and saw Jim just turning his saddle horse loose. He looked up when I hollered out, "Howdy old-timer." Jim looked real surprised and said, "Well, you old son of a . . . ! Where do you think you're going to?" So I told him I was heading my horse for Barkerville to have a look around for a day or two.

I hadn't seen him for around two years — since we were breaking horses and haying at the Gang — so we had lots to talk about. I turned Pilot loose in the saddle horse pasture and after a darned good supper of salt pork and beans, and fried buckaroo spuds and hot coffee and hot biscuit, and a couple of cigarettes, I rolled into some extra blankets Jim had there, figuring I'd had a hell of a good day. I sure didn't need any rocking in the cradle to get a real sound sleep that night.

Morning came rolling in with the old sun just ashining through the cabin window, and I heard Jim fussing around the stove and mixing up a batch of hotcakes which soon enough we tied into with some bacon, syrup and coffee.

Jim was sure glad to see me, and I was tickled to see him again. We talked the usual cow range gossip that all cowboys enjoy and he suggested I'd better rest up my horse for a day or so before going on and he'd show me around, which sounded good to me.

It didn't take me very long to see that Jim was looking after a much bigger spread on the north side of the Chilcotin than I had down at the old Crow's Bar. The Gang had 1,400 steers on that north side which Jim was responsible for while I had only around 550 spayed heifers on the Crow's Bar end. Of course I knew that the company put about five hundred heifers each year into their cow herd for replacement stock so that, to my mind, accounted for a lot of the difference — but that Chilcotin steer pasture sure looked like a grass paradise to me.

Jim said to me we'd saddle up and take a little ride to see some friends of his and have noon with them, so we caught up a little sorrel mare called Dollie out of the pasture for me to ride, while Pilot really filled his belly with grass.

We rode on down the hog's back to the bridge, which he told me was called Chilcotin Falls, and up the river about half a mile was a little ranch right alongside the river which was owned by two young English fellows, named Farwell and Gerald Blenkinsop, these boys owning a small bunch of cows and growing real good alfalfa hay, and looked like they made a good living there.

After we'd had a good dinner and a smoke, Jim and I started back for the cabin. After we'd crossed over the bridge we noticed some fresh wheel tracks and saddle horse tracks just below the bridge, so we followed up the tracks and a few minutes later we came on to a little tent, and a campfire outside the tent, and an Indian "klootch" with three kids playing around the tent, and a fair-sized white man with them.

Jim knew the outfit real well and we had a half hour's talk with them. The white man was an educated Englishman who spoke English with a very high Oxford accent, and was a remittance man who had five hundred dollars allowance sent to him every three months from old England by his folks back there. The Indian queen who was called "Crazy Jennie" seemed to be just what "His Lordship" needed out here in the wild and woolly Chilcotin country. It seemed like she was a good cook and a good worker and probably a good bed partner — so it was just made to order all around.

This Indian gal must have been real smart to learn and observe things because she spoke somewhat with an Oxford accent too — which I guess must have sounded like home to the high-class Englishman.

Crazy Jennie had these three kids, each one from a different pappy — one little girl had real brown hair and a lot of freckles, and Jim said this bright little girl's pappy was a pretty good Scotchman who had ranged around the Chilcotin some in previous years. The oldest of the two boys with her was a full-blooded Indian boy who might have had a pretty good dad by the look of him. The second boy had real kinky black hair and Jim told me he was the son of a coloured gentleman who had lived down the river and had died a few years previously.

All in all, they presented quite a picture there on the bank of the Chilcotin and Jim and I climbed up on our horses and started up the long hog's back trail to the cabin and when we stopped awhile to give our horses a little breather, Jim turned in his saddle and said to me, "Harry, if I can just put a Californian in that little bunch down there I'll sure as hell be able to start a show." I told him I figured it was a very worthwhile objective.

I don't know how this Cariboo Country would ever have got going unless these old-timers — some of them afoot, others with some sort of a horse or a team — had not started with an Indian gal, or klootch as they were called, and as they settled on creeks and flats along the rivers, and by endless hard work and effort, carved themselves out a little home and ranch, and raised up a family of halfbreed kids.

I have noticed that these Indian gals never had very much at any time and when one of them took up with a white man she lived a lot better than in an Indian Reserve. They always looked up to the man as being the boss at all times, and few if any white girls would take the rugged life, and having to get along with very little, like the Indian gals did. There were little or no legal troubles because very few actually were ever legally married to any white man they lived with, so if any trouble came along and a "split the blankets" situation arose, there were no divorce cases or pocket-book breaking alimony business in that deal. The Indian gal shopped around and probably picked up another fellow and the white boy generally rustled himself up another partner.

A great friend of mine, and a real top number one figuring hound, once told me that it was his "idee" that an Indian gal lived with a white man for his money and better grub and clothes and that she lived with an Indian for straight love of him. Once in a while she'd live with a Chinaman out of plumb curiosity but, by and large, I've seen a lot of darned good handy Indian gals in my time, and in those days white gals were as scarce as hen's teeth and awful hard to get, and what few there were, were scattered over the ranges and had more beaux after them than would patch old Hell a mile, and then some.

Jim and I got back up to the cabin and after awhile he cooked supper while I split some firewood and packed some water to the cabin. When we had finished supper, the days and the daylight being long, Jim said, "Harry, we'll take a ride over to Beecher's." Beecher's was near Riske Creek which was only about seven or eight miles away, and not far to ride on a long summer's evening.

So we rode over to Beecher's, which was a general store, a hotel with a bar in it, and a little ranch operation with it. However,

Beecher's was quite a trading spot for the ranchers around and the Indians from the reserve. It was also a post office and on the main road from the Cariboo Road to the Chilcotin district, so there were sometimes quite a few travellers stayed at Beecher's, on the weekly stage line which ran through the Chilcotin as far as Kleena Kleene. Beecher himself was an old-timer who had originally come from England and had settled there, and had started his trading store and did considerable trade with the Indians in furs and sold a lot of booze over his bar.

Jim made me known to all and sundry in the bar, and I had several rounds of "O-B-Joyful" with the boys and looking around I failed to see Jim. However, I met up with a very agreeable man called Tommy Armstrong, who had been running a little bunch of cows about forty miles to the west of Beecher's. Tommy told me he was going to ride over to the company cabin that night, so we decided we'd ride back together as I couldn't find hide nor hair of Jim Ragan when it came time to go. So after I had ginned up the boys for another round of booze or two, Tommy and I started back on the trail to the cabin with a bottle of hootch apiece tied behind our saddles and feeling no pain at all. We started out just as the last string of daylight was fading out into the darkness and rode along the trail to the cabin, talking about this and that, and every so often we'd take a little nip out of the bottle, tied on behind our saddles, and it was not very long before it was pitch dark and I noticed, or thought I did anyway, that we had ridden off the trail someway, so I tied my bridle lines together and let them hang loose, figuring that this Dollie mare I was riding would find her way straight to the gate on the trail, at the steer range pasture — but it didn't turn out that way. As we came in the darkness to a small lake Dollie walked eight times around that lake followed, of course, by Tommy on his horse. So after the eighth time around I said to Tommy, "That's enough, we'll just tie up our horses to these cottonwood trees and wait a few hours till daylight." This we did, and I groped around in the dark and found some dead cottonwood twigs and made a little fire, and we sat down and talked and cat-napped a little by the fire, taking a little jolt of booze every so often to keep up the circulation and our bellies warm. After some considerable time the daylight began peeping its way in and that grand old haymaker, a nice warm sun, rose up over the mountains to the east of us.

Sure enough, the gate going in to the Gang Ranch steer range was only about half a mile from this lake we'd camped out at, so my little Dollie mare must have figured she was pretty near home when she went round and round that lake so often as she did with me. It didn't take us very long to get through that gate and down to the cabin, where we found Jim Ragan in bed, so I made a fire in the stove as I was a little chilly. What with getting thawed out by the hot fire, and nicely wozey with all those snorts I'd been having and not being used to it, I got higher than a hoot owl, and staggered off to bed and slept like a dead man.

The next day early I started out on Pilot to ride out towards Soda Creek, and I made around thirty miles that day, and stayed at a ranch on Meldrum Creek, close to the Fraser, which was owned by a gentleman called Major Richards, who sure made me very welcome, and the day following I rode in to Soda Creek, having crossed the Fraser on a ferry at that place.

Next day I rode Pilot right along the Cariboo Road up towards the little town of Quesnel. It was about sixty miles from Soda Creek to Quesnel and that was two easy days' ride for me and Pilot — there being different ranches and stopping places every five to fifteen miles along that Cariboo Road.

I was beginning to get more or less convinced as I went along that the country along the Cariboo from Soda Creek north was not much of a "cow country" as I knew cow ranges — so I rode on up ten miles on the Barkerville road from Quesnel, and stayed overnight with an old French Canadian named Jerry Gravelle who was a very old-timer in that area. He gave me a whole pile of good information in regards to this Upper Cariboo — it was a country of mines and timber and no signs of any worthwhile cow range. Anyone running cows in that thick jungle of timber would pretty near need a bell on every hoof of them to find them, except when the snow was laying on the ground. After meditating on this matter, I figured I'd start south again in the morning and get back again to Crow's Bar which was around one hundred and ninety miles away.

So in the morning I bid good luck to this kindly old French-Canadian voyageur and his pretty little half-breed daughter, and I headed old Pilot for Crow's Bar — stopping at Quesnel overnight. That evening I was sitting outside the hotel on the verandah and I noticed a very old man with a long white beard sitting there. He said his name was MacClean and that in the gold rush around 1860, on a place called Lightning Creek near Barkerville, he had shovelled out thirty-six bucks worth of gold nuggets for days on end.

Next morning I was all ready to light out for Soda Creek when a young fellow stepped up to me and asked me if I would sell my horse Pilot. He said he would give me $200 for that saddle horse. Of course I told him that Pilot was a Gang Ranch horse and I had no right to sell him, even for such a fancy price.

This young fellow turned out to be the famous Dr. Baker, who was afterwards a real household word in that upper Cariboo. I heard several different stories of Dr. Baker operating on guys' appendixes on the kitchen table — miles away from any sort of help — so I'll bet the doctor was just the ticket for that sort of scattered country.

I did notice half a dozen pretty good layouts between Quesnel and Soda Creek but they looked like good mixed farms to me, not cattle ranches, and I was glad when I crossed back over on the ferry at Soda Creek and headed my horse to the Chilcotin pasture where once again I stayed overnight with Jim Ragan. In the morning, wishing him "So long," I crossed the Chilcotin and over the trail to the Gang and next day down the river to Crow's Bar and home. I'd had a good trip and a change of scenery and seeing different folks, so I was ready to go to work.

I had just got back from my trip about a couple of weeks when Tommy Derbe — who had his ranch on the north end of the Crow's Bar pasture — sold out the ranch and cattle to a man named Henry Koster and a young man named Joe Smith who was the second son of the old pioneer, Joe Smith, who started and owned the Clinton Hotel in around 1864.

Henry Koster was the son of a German aristocratic family who emigrated to this Cariboo Country in the days of the Barkerville gold rush — and afterwards took up the Alkali Lake Ranch. He was married to an English lady, and was a man of great ability and had a very far-seeing head on him. Not only was he a good cattleman, but he was what the experts call "a man of good executive ability." The ranch he purchased from Tom Derbe was just a stepping stone from which in after years he built up and owned the Canoe Creek Company's ranch and the Empire Valley holdings.

Henry and young Joe Smith, as he was affectionately called, and myself all formed a permanent and lasting respect and friendship for each other for many years — until both Henry and Joe crossed over on that "One Way Trail."

I was not anyways sorry at all to see Tom Derbe sell out his ranch because I had never even got a thank you out of him for the many odds and ends of things I had done for him at different times. It was a good thing for him that he did sell out because if a man owns a ranch and doesn't ride around his cows kind of regular, and lets his calves run around unbranded, sooner or later someone else may brand them for him — not with his brand at all but their brand, which will soon run a man out of cows.

Summertime was in full swing in 1914 when I was sitting on a little bit of a porch on the Crow's Bar cabin after supper, smoking and watching the sun spreading his evening rays on the mountains, when I saw a rider coming down the trail and as he got closer I saw it was my boss, Andy Stobie. Of course I jumped up and started the fire going to get him a bite of supper. He stayed overnight with me and I proceeded to give him a detailed account of the progress I had made at Crow's Bar.

I told the boss of a lot of things I'd done — how I'd put up a saddle horse pasture, and another log cabin to hold supplies and extra equipment, which was very badly needed. I had rebuilt and renovated the barn, and had increased my horse hay from five to fifteen tons, and had made a ditch about a mile and a half long to turn a rush of snow water each spring down into a fair-sized lake which in turn freshened up the water for the cattle to drink, and on top of that, I had faithfully looked after the cattle with very few losses.

Andy listened to me very closely and said, "Aye mon Harry, ye've done very well," so I was pleased and glad to hear he was satisfied with my work.

It appeared that Andy Stobie had been notified to appear as a juryman at the Clinton Cariboo Assizes, which at that time were held once a year in Clinton, and he asked me if I would like to come to Clinton with him for a few days. I at once agreed that I'd like to go on the trip. Next day Stobie and I rode to Clinton, getting there around five o'clock in the afternoon and I stabled both saddle horses in the big old barn across the street from the Clinton

Hotel — Andy getting a room for us in the hotel with two beds in it. The town was very full of people during those few days of the Assizes, as a considerable number had been notified for jury service — which was imperative for them to attend — and I met many folks from all over the Cariboo.

There was a great deal of hitting the bottle every day in the hotel and Andy Stobie was generosity itself with his own money — far too generous for his own good — and his cry, "Everybody up," several times a day and night was replied to by all and sundry at the bar. I didn't drink much booze in those years, and I took it on myself to be Stobie's "Man Friday." When he would finally get pretty full I'd always be sticking around close to help him up to bed, and to be sure I had a pretty stout eye-opener for him first thing in the morning.

I took care of our saddle horses every day and would sometimes get an hour or two listening to the court cases — which were many and varied — ranging all the way from cow stealing to murder trials, and a rape case.

The Clinton Hotel certainly did a roaring business in those years with its never-ending string of travellers and freight teams up and down the road. The bar did a big business in selling liquor, many of the boys waking up in the morning after the night before with big hang-overs, a sick stomach and a flattened-out pocket book.

The Assizes got wound up and, after several days in Clinton, Stobie and I stepped up on our horses and headed for home. After riding 25 miles as far as Meadow Lake, Andy rode on to the Gang and I turned off on a trail leading on down to Upper Big Bar Creek and from there on to Big Bar Mountain and the Crow's Bar pasture. I was pleased to get back to the cabin after the few days of different folks I'd met from many points in the Cariboo. After I'd turned my horse out in the saddle horse pasture and had cooked my supper, I sat down on the porch and watched the golden sun settling down behind the high mountains away west of the river. I never did get tired of looking at those sunsets — the whole country looked like it really was a peaceful, quiet and grand picture of natural beauty.

Chapter 7

A Long Tough Ride

Most generally, unless I was off riding the range, or gathering cattle, I'd ride over to a little ranch on the main stage road which was called "The Mountain House" — afterwards named Jesmond. It was then, and up to the present time, owned and operated by a family called Coldwell who are certainly one of the most respected old-time families of that Big Bar country.

There was a post office at Jesmond and every Wednesday evening the weekly mail stage, which was carried by horses in those years, came into the Coldwell's and stayed overnight there while en route to Dog Creek and Alkali Lake. As it was only about eight miles from the Crow's Bar cabin I used to ride over and get letters, if I had any.

I well remember around the second week in August 1914, the news came to Big Bar Creek of the start of World War I and, with little or no communication with the outside, we only heard vague and hazy reports of the big advances in Belgium and France — of Kaiser Bill's rough, tough and well-trained armies.

I used to ride up the river trail to the Gang Ranch about once in every six weeks and in the summer months when it was real hot all day long, I'd wait until the moon was full and then start out for the Gang, and ride nearly all night when it was cool and easy riding on your horse. The moon and the stars both ashining bright as a new silver dollar and I'd arrive at the gang around 4:00 a.m. and would snooze away in some corner of the bunkhouse till the breakfast bell rang.

I was getting fifty dollars a month and my board all year around — running the Crow's Bar spread for the Gang. I always sat on a good saddle and had a lot of good cowhand rigging — chaps, spurs, boots, rope, bridle and a hackamore. I had bought two saddle horses for myself, so with my own two horses and the two the Gang supplied me with, I always had a fresh horse any day I needed one. A fellow doing quite a bit of riding needs two or three horses at least, because riding one horse day after day makes the horse loggy and leg weary. When you want a quick jumper or a real smart run, you just ain't got it on a half tired out horse.

Along about the last week in August of 1914 on one of my trips to the Gang my friend, MacIntyre, with whom I had formed a close friendship, asked me if I would stay over a day and help him, and another of the boys, run in the saddle horse bunch from out in the big pasture. We had a long hard run to bunch up them saddle horses. They'd sure run quite a hickory and were plumb full of hellery, but we stayed with them and finally ran them into a smaller pasture close to the Gang Ranch buildings.

It rained all day and it was close to evening when Mac and I were riding towards the Gang and we were pretty damp and wet, so Mac said, "I'll beat you to the barn, Harry." I said, "You will like hell," and we started to race our horses. Mac was beating me a little when on turning a corner, going hell bent for election, my horse's feet slipped out from under him in the soft greasy mud, and down he came with my right foot underneath him. A red-hot pain shot up from my ankle and I just couldn't bear my weight on it.

Mac came back looking for me and helped me to get on my horse. I flopped off somehow at the bunkhouse and one of the boys cut my riding boot loose and the old ankle was sure swelled up.

I got my ankle in cold water, then bandaged it up real tight with some spare cloth. For three weeks I sat around the bunkhouse nursing up this broken ankle. During this time I rigged myself up a crutch which helped me to get around pretty fair and after the three weeks were past I decided if I had a real gentle horse I'd make the thirty-three miles down the river trail to Crow's Bar, crutch and all.

I hobbled around all that fall, but I managed to round up the cattle and get my winter's grub down from the Gang, and also get set for winter. During that winter when I had to ride down among the cattle on the winter range, I sure used to ride kind of slow and careful like when it came to riding over a slick icy patch, even on a good sharp shod horse.

The spring of 1915 came rolling along and in early March I rode up the Gang and brought down some 230 head of heifer calves and they were spayed in early May. I made the annual round of the eighteen miles of fence around Crow's Bar and looked after the cattle in the usual range riding, and more and more I was getting kind of riled up by the news of our boys in France having a hell of a time to hold their own against the go-getting battle-trained ruthless German armies.

I had a white-haired mother living in England in those years and I had not seen her for over eight years. In letters to me she would mention relations of mine who were in action with the British forces in France, and so the thought came sifting in to my mind that it was just naturally up to me to leave my job at the Crow's Bar and go join up with the Canadians, just as soon as the cattle were rounded up in the fall and the most important jobs of the year were done.

I rode up the river in early August of that year, 1915, and told my old boss, Andy Stobie, that I guess I'd have to quit somewheres around Christmas as I figured I'd have to go and join our army till the war got finished up anyway.

Stobie listened while I told him the story and the only remark he made was, "I shall miss you to beat hell, but I guess it can't be helped, mon."

That evening I saw an old Indian, called Indian Jimmy, ride in to the Gang and he and Andy were engaged in a long session of talking back and forth. The next morning, right after breakfast, Andy Stobie said, "Harry, my monny, I want you to make a long ride for me today."

I asked him, "Where to?"

Andy said, "I want you to ride to Clinton, mon, and tell Frank Aikens to get up here as fast as he can. You must make it there today, and tell Frank to come at once."

It appeared that Indian Jimmy had come riding down Gaspard Creek and had seen a white man sitting by a tent, with a smoke fire under a piece of meat hanging from a limb of a good-sized fir tree. The old Indian at once figured that this white man had killed a Gang Ranch critter and was smoking some of the hind-quarter — no doubt intending to make some jerked meat, which will keep for a long time, so he had ridden on down to the Gang to tell Stobie.

There were no cars, telephones or what-have-you in the Gang Ranch country those days, and you either rode a saddle horse or drove a team and light rig — or else you went afoot — there was no other choice.

Clinton was 73 miles away from the Gang and I knew at once that I was in for a long ride before it got dark. I knew it had to be done and I was kind of sure if I took some short cuts on the trail that I could save my horse at least five miles. So I threw my saddle on a very fast-walking little bay gelding named Grasshopper, and left my horse at the Gang. This little bay Grasshopper was sure a bugger to walk — just like sitting in a rocking chair, as mile after mile he kept up that fast walk. I rode down the river trail and figured I'd got 33 miles of the 70-odd done when I stopped to let the little bay feed for an hour or so while I lay on the grass, biting down some tough beef and cold hotcakes, and gulped down some water out of a spring. By this time it was time to catch the gelding and up I stepped to make the last lap.

I took a short-cut trail and saved myself five miles or more. My horse never changed his fast walk and about six-thirty that night I rode into Kelly Lake with just eleven more miles to get to Clinton. A friend of mine named Barney Johnson was running the ranch at Kelly Lake and he got me a bite of supper and offered to lend me his saddle horse to ride to Clinton, so I told him, "Barney, you lend me your horse and I'll ride in to Clinton and I'll be back tonight, but it will be kind of late." My friend, Barney, said it was fine with him anyway.

I finished eating my supper and clumb up on Barney's big bay saddle horse and headed for Clinton. I told Frank Aikens the story. Frank was the constable for the area, which was sure enough a real man-sized country, real country, real far and wide, and he told me he'd start out riding first thing in the morning. He had no car, in fact the only place you saw a car those years was on the Cariboo Road — not many at that. What cars I did see were blowing a real heavy black smoke at their hind ends and noisy as a carload of monkeys.

My message delivered to the "Bull" I stepped up on Barney's big bay and rode back to Kelly Lake. I was getting a little tired, particularly as Barney's horse was sure a straight-shouldered, big-footed snoozer whose hoofs were bigger round than a wash basin. This made him rougher than sitting on a wagon load of rocks. I have always noticed that any horse that takes over a number 2 size shoe is no good as a saddle horse and should be looking through a collar — making his living pulling a plough.

Well, I tumbled into bed at Kelly Lake around midnight and felt that I had done a good day's ride for sure. Seventy-nine miles is a real ride in a day for any old, or young, cowboy. In after years I made a similar ride, but I'll come to that later in my story.

On the next day I rode back from Kelly Lake to the Crow's Bar cabin and a few days later I rode on up to the Gang and knew I'd have to leave the little Grasshopper horse there as Mac would sure want him. At the Gang, I found out that Frank Aikens had been there, and that the white man smoking the meat was a prospector who had killed an unbranded wild cayuse and was smoking a ham of horsemeat, not beef at all, so I'd had my long ride all for nothing. Anyway it was a good thing for the prospector, because if it had been beef he'd have got five years in the calaboose probably, sitting in the shade, with a suit of black arrows to wear. Cow stealing in any form sure did bring a pretty stiff jolt for anyone caught and convicted at it — in those years. It seems to me today the judge lets them off far too easy, with a little two-three months holiday in a jail, just enough to give the cow-thief a good rest and maybe breakfast in bed, with peach melba for dessert.

I rounded up the cattle that fall and decided I would strike off and volunteer for this military service. I was not alone locally in this decision as there were six other boys besides myself who all had the same notion. The day after New Year's in 1916 saw me hang up my saddle at the Gang Ranch. I turned over my job to a fellow called Bert Barrow and after a farewell dance at Canoe Creek Ranch house, which lasted for three nights and was atttended by away over a hundred people, whites and Indians alike, they all wished us godspeed and we started for Vancouver in 40° below zero weather.

I sure hated to leave the Gang and old Crow's Bar, which had become such a home for me. My grand old friend, Andy Stobie, shook me by the hand and told me, "God damn it, Harry mon, I'll be waiting for you when you come home." I knew full well it just had to be done, 'cause any young man who would stand idly by and see his country really up agin it for help, don't look like much of a real fellow to me — or his country either.

There were seven of us all told: Eddie Haller and Alec Haller, both sons of the Big Bar old-timer, Joe Haller; Johnnie Hartman and Sam Kersey, who were both raised around Big Bar; John Bill Bunnage, ferry man at Big Bar; Harold Willshire, who was ranch hand from Dog Creek; and myself, Harry Marriott, cowhand and Crow's Bar manager for the Gang Ranch.

After a few days jollification around Vancouver — on one occasion we had our recruiting officer standing on top of the bar in a hotel, singing "Annie Laurie" and higher than a hoot-owl — we enlisted in the 158th Duke of Connaught's Own Regiment in Vancouver and we all took oath to serve in His Majesty's Canadian Armed Forces for the duration of the war, and six months after if necessary, and to serve in any capacity that His Majesty's Canadian Forces would require of us. That oath sure covered a whole pile — believe me.

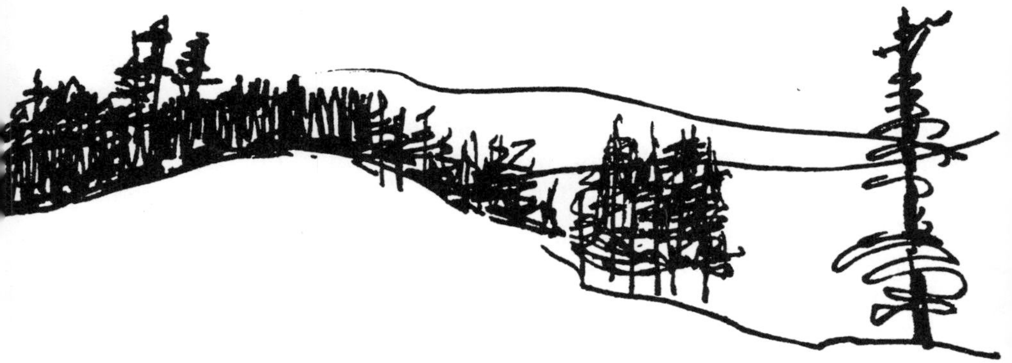

Chapter 8

Picking a Homestead

I WILL NOT DWELL ON, nor relate here my experiences while serving in that grand and capable army — known as the Canadian Expeditionary Force — in the days of World War I. I was hit by shrapnel a couple of times, but not seriously, and I was scared to death a million times, but that was a daily diet for most all of the boys in action — and the Canucks were a real active nightmare to the "Heinies" on many occasions, and I felt kind of proud and glad that I'd been some help to our Grand Old Canada.

After three years and two months service I took my discharge in New Westminster, B.C., and threaded my way back to the big old Cariboo, and the Gang Ranch, with a longing and a thankfulness in my heart that I was returning to the big wide-open spaces and the mountains and valleys of our Southern Cariboo.

It was a land of white-faced cows, and kind-faced people, and the old familiar cry of "Howdy, neighbour, light off your horse and come in," which was almost always the rule in that sparsely settled country. By and large, I don't think anyone was a stranger longer than thirty seconds in our country in those years gone by.

Even today it has not changed a great deal, but the coming of good roads, cars and trucks have narrowed down, by hours and days, the time it took to travel by horse or wagon — all of which has proved to be a blessing of so-called civilization. In fact, I've often wondered if there isn't a danger of being too over-civilized, with all these latest fancy gadgets there is around nowadays. I've always noticed that a lean hound-dog always rustles better than a fat one, and same goes for human beings. If they get too fat and prosperous, chances are they can't stand a real rough spell, not worth a damn.

I found things at the Gang very much the same as when I left. My old boss, Andy Stobie, was sure glad to see me, and Mac and most of the boys still there — also some new faces. After staying a few days at the Gang, Stobie told me I'd better ride down the river and take over my old job at Crow's Bar again. So I gathered up my saddle and outfit and started down the river trail, riding a bay saddle horse called Whisper. I reached the old home at Crow's Bar along late in the afternoon and felt real happy to be back again at the old cabin.

There was little or no change at Crow's Bar, or at Big Bar Creek either. Some of the folks on the creek had been thinned out by the flu which struck Big Bar in the fall of 1918. Some of the dry farms on Big Bar Mountain seemed to me to have been getting a lot tougher, with dry summers and hot warm winds, and grasshoppers were much more frequent than before — and all these things were pretty rough medicine in the game of raising crops and feed for their few head of cattle.

Of the seven of us boys who had left the Big Bar country, only one didn't return. Little Johnny Hartman was killed in action in August 1918, but the rest of us more or less settled down again to our former ways of life. I had one hell of a time getting settled down again, for a matter of a month or two, after getting back to Crow's Bar. It was a big change from the rush, roar of action of army life — the excitement and high pitch of armies in action, and the "eat, drink and be merry, because tomorrow you may die" atmosphere for quite a long spell. All these were a considerable change to a set-up of being alone most of the time, and being my own boss, with decisions to make once more.

However, I applied the only solution possible to tide over the problems that beset any and each of us — and that was to work like hell, and get too interested and too tired at the end of the day to let any thoughts or meditations bother you at all. I had a lot of thoughts and ideas — more notions in my head than a dog has fleas — in those days following my discharge from the service. The most persistent one was that it was time I was trying to get a little start and a home of my own somewhere.

I could see no earthly chance of any promotion at the Gang. The urge to have a place of my own with a little bunch of good cows, and some hay to winter them on, and a little bit of range for them — maybe a chance to find a real good long-haired partner, if I could find one — all these things looked pretty good to me. The first thing anyone who wants something real bad has to do, is to make a start and bow your neck towards winning the game.

In my several years of riding the range, gathering up the Gang Ranch beef, I had seen and often ridden over a fair-sized flat which was lying on the north side of Big Bar Lake. It was only about four miles from the head waters of Big Bar Creek, which was plumb full of large spruce swamps. This flat covered at least 80 to 100 acres of fairly good ground — dotted here and there with a few jack-pines and poplar patches of timber — and while some parts of the flat were tinged with alkali, I felt that quite a lot of hay could be grown on this flat if I could get an irrigation ditch from the creek.

I rode up to the Big Bar Lake again on a Sunday in early June of 1919 and I borrowed a good carpenter's level from my good friend Harry Coldwell, of Jesmond, and riding to the creek, I got off my horse and started taking sights along the level. This made me feel real sure that there was around ten to twelve feet of a fall in the mile or so distance from the creek to the flat — and that would mean I could take an irrigation ditch from the creek and run it out on to the main flat for irrigation. I figured my ditch would hit the creek about a mile from the head of Big Bar Lake.

An irrigation ditch should have a smooth even-gaited flow if you want to get the best, and a fall of eight feet to the mile, or one-quarter inch to every twelve feet is just about right for a good irrigation ditch. I had to be sure I could get the water on to the flat, because no water is no good, and means a lot of skimpy crops on hay fields in most years. The good Lord never did send us much rainfall from Ashcroft up to Soda Creek, on both sides of this old Cariboo Road.

You can grow rye hay in quite a few places without any irrigation, as rye is a hardy tough old hombre, but as a hay for livestock, it is just better than no hay at all, and in the winter rye-hay will make a better chunk of manure than eating snowballs.

On the 19th day of June 1919, I stepped up on my saddle horse and rode into the Clinton Government Office and filed a homestead claim on the Big Bar Lake flat, and I applied for a six month's leave-of-absence before I had to really start living on it. I returned to the Crow's Bar pasture knowing that, "win, lose or draw," I'd got the first start-off of a home, so I carefully started to save what little money I had, and to hang on to my wages.

One day around the last week in June 1919, I had been out riding around a fence, and making sure there were no broken wires, or the fence down, and I had just started to make a fire in the cabin stove when I heard a noise outside, and looking out I saw a friend of mine named Frank Ellis tying his saddle horse up to my hitching rack — a matter of about forty feet out from the cabin. Frank Ellis was the overall manager of the B.C. Cattle Co., which was the Canoe Creek Ranch, and he and the Ellis family at that time were considerable owners in the spread.

After I had fed him a bite we sat down on the cabin porch and rolled a couple of cigarettes and starting talking about the range grass and the cow business in general. Frank came to the point of his little visit to me by offering me a job as ranch foreman for the Canoe Creek layout. I meditated for several minutes before I answered him. I knew I could handle the job and be able to get some work out of the boys, so I told Ellis that I could come, but only for a limited time as I had to make my start at Big Bar Lake, and I agreed that I'd take on the job until the end of December.

At that time the Canoe Creek Ranch was a very compact, easy-run and well-operated layout, and in those years the ranch ran around twelve hundred head of white-faced Herefords. It had around twenty miles of good winter range along the Fraser. It was, and is to this day, a real fine cattle spread and I had many associations with that good ranch over many years. Sure enough I bid "So long" to the Crow's Bar cabin and to my old friend, Andy Stobie, at the Gang and rode over to Canoe Creek which was around twenty-odd miles from Crow's Bar.

The ranch always had an entirely Indian crew, with a Chinese cook and two Chinese irrigators. The Indian boys mostly belonged to the Indian village or rancherie, which was only about three-quarters of a mile away from the main ranch house at Canoe Creek. I got along very well with these Indian boys, they were a real capable bunch as far as ranch work goes, and most of them quiet and slow-spoken. All of them could speak English after a fashion, but their native tongue was Shuswap, which is their tribal form of Indian language. While none of them ever seemed to have much ambition — when compared to our ideas — and none that I ever knew wanted to accept leadership or responsibility, yet they were good workers while they worked, and in practical range work and handling range cattle, they could hold their own in the cow business. Like every class of human beings on earth, some were far ahead of others, however, I can certainly say from my own experience that they were a pretty good bunch to lead and to get along with in a ranch operation.

It was in these years that we had the arrival of a newcomer to our Cariboo, in the form of a railroad called the Pacific Great Eastern Railway which is owned by the Province of British Columbia. This P.G.E., or "Please Go Easy" as some smart joshers called it, started its way at Squamish on Howe Sound down on the Pacific, and had pushed its way up as far as Williams Lake and Quesnel where it stayed for years before completion. Practically speaking, this railroad "started nowhere and finished at nowhere" but it did offer an outlet for the ranchers to ship to the Vancouver market, and load on a barge from Squamish on down. This barge trip made a big bunch of the cattle get seasick on the barge, which sure made them look pretty ragged when they were unloaded at the packing house, which did not help the cattlemen any too much as regards prices.

However, today the P.G.E. has been completed, and has proved to be a blessing for the ranch owners. It has opened up a lot of country in the Peace River areas, and has provided a good outlet for the Cariboo's latest industry, the logging and saw-milling of a lot of lumber.

I mind in those early years — with its newly made grades and tracks — the comings and goings of the old P.G.E. trains were largely a big gambling problem. A great friend of mine told me that the only way he could be plumb sure of the arrival of the train heading for Clinton, was the fact that one conductor had a long buckskin-coloured hound-dog, who would be coyote-trotting along the track ahead of the train a mile or so — his nose to the ground and stopping every so often to smell and sprinkle the stumps along the railroad track. However, today our Cariboo railroad is sure a well-run, modern and efficient concern, and it will hold its own in any man's country.

With the coming of the P.G.E. there ended the grand old freight-hauling days from Ashcroft up, with the teams and wagons, and the travel on the Cariboo Road was greatly reduced — until in after years when the road up the Fraser Canyon was completed. It brought a lot of real big competition between freight trucks and the P.G.E.

December 1919 came rolling along and I had to leave my job as straw-boss at Canoe Creek, so I headed my saddle horse for the Big Bar Lake homestead. Earlier that fall I had made a deal with Grant Lee, who lived on Big Bar Creek, to put me up a log cabin 16 x 20 on the lake homestead.

I bought an old cook-stove from a real kindly and friendly old couple named George and Maggie Watt, who lived about ten miles away at the east end of Beaver Dam Lake, and with a few months' supply of grub — very plain grub at that — a good double-bitted axe and a crosscut-saw, I settled down to put in my first winter on the homestead. I had saved up about sixteen hundred dollars out of my wages and war gratuities, so I figured I'd eat for a while any-how, and try to get going.

I had a neighbour that winter who lived four miles away down on the Creek at the west end of the lake. Like me, he was a bache-lor and I made a dicker with him to feed my saddle horse all win-ter as I had no hay of any kind at that time. I knew my horse would not last out the winter pawing in the snow for grass, and a lot of snowballs mixed up with it. I set my mind on cutting jack-pine fence rails, with a view to getting a rail fence around the homestead as soon as the bare ground showed up in the spring, so every day, snow or otherwise, except on a Sunday, I used to tramp across the opening half a mile or more to some jack-pine timber, axe in hand and saw on my shoulder. When evening started to show up and the sun dipped down behind the mountain on the south side of the lake, I generally had 130 to 160 fence rails cut and piled up.

Sometimes I used to have to waddle through fairly deep snow-drifts going back and forth across the flats, but I had my mind made up to get the rails cut before the winter was over. It was a long winter and every night I'd come into the cabin, which was right close to the lake, and I'd get the fire going first, then take off my wet socks and overalls and hang them up behind the stove and put on some dry socks and old dry overalls. I'd start to cook my supper — mostly rice, beans and fried pork and dough-dodger bread — with a little saucerful of boiled prunes to top off the meal. I had little variety, but that kind of good plain grub gave me the necessary wallop to cut rails all day. My spuds froze in the cabin during a 40° below zero spell — so I threw them out in the snow, and then thawed out a few every time I'd put on a mess of spuds, but they sure did taste terrible bitter, so I didn't include spuds too long in the daily grub.

After my supper I'd wash my dishes up, and sit beside the cook-stove for a while with a sort of satisfied feeling that each day I was doing something worthwhile and around nine o'clock I'd hit the hay, as the old bedtime saying goes. I had a few old magazines which I read many times that long winter, and I had a little Bible that my old mother had given me when I left England in 1907. I read the New Testament part several times.

As the spring came along in 1920 the snow started melting and ran off the sidehills and slopes into the lake. Bare ground showed up and the crows were the first birds to arrive but they were soon followed by a half dozen kinds, such as blackbirds, martins, and the old camp-robbers. There was a bunch of prairie-chicken birds used to mate on a small knoll real close to the lake, and their billing and cooing and bowing to each other back and forth, reminded me some of a square dance.

My neighbour boy, Billy Megaitt, pulled out for the Okanagan country where he had been raised, in the spring of 1920, and I rented his little meadow and bought his two horses, harness and wagon. One of the horses was sure a fine old work horse named Brownie — and the other horse, I called him Raven. I had to break him to ride and to drive, doing all this by myself, and ten miles away from anyone. I used a lot of patience, time and skill to break this little short-coupled colt, and he turned out to be an all-star horse for me for many years.

About the first week in May of that year, my two great Indian friends from Canoe Creek Reserve, Louie Tisnashet and Cowboy Joe, with their wives and two or three other young Indians, all came over to the lake and helped me to haul the fence rails and put up the fence around the homestead, which took about three weeks. I paid them for the job and they started back to the reserve. I figured that the grass would start to grow inside the fence as there would be no stock in there for a while, but later that spring I purchased seven heifers from a fellow living over twenty miles away and put them in the new fenced pasture.

That winter I had applied to the Brand Commissioner in Victoria to take out a cattle and horse brand. I applied for the brand O K on the left ribs for cattle, and O K on the left hip for horses — and that brand was mine until the O K Ranch was sold in 1950. I never knew or expected in those far-off days that the expression "it's O K" would become such an all-round household saying as it has become since those days.

There was a pretty good log house, a barn and corral on the little meadow I had rented, and the creek bubbled along on its way to the Fraser only a few yards from the house. I got to studying on the matter and decided that I would move down from the lake cabin and live at the meadow for a while at least. There being no fence of any kind around the meadow, I began at once to cut rails to make a fence around the meadow also.

I got to be a real number one axe man, and cutting fence rails was just duck-soup for me. I'd ride out about once a week to get my mail — if any — and I'd take the team and wagon to Clinton in the spring and get myself several months' grub on the one trip, always being sure that I had plenty of tobacco because to anyone who smokes at all, it is sure a real Hell to be out of tobacco.

Every spring, somewhere around the latter end of April, the Kamloops trout used to run up the creek from a lake lower down called Little Bar Lake and they would lay their eggs in the gravelly and rocky shallows along Big Bar Creek. As I had a gravelly fast-running water strip right outside my door at the little meadow, I used to eat fish, fish and more fish, for the best part of three weeks every spring. The creek would just be alive with them and I could roll up my shirt sleeve away high and gently slide my hand under the bank of the creek, and I'd feel a fish's tail with the tips of my fingers, and gently run my fingers underneath his belly till I reached the gills and then I'd make a quick squeeze with my fingers pressed tight in his gills, and the trout would be mine. I'll sure say that fried fish and fried spuds makes a real good meal for anybody. I have heard that in Scotland this kind of catching fish is called "guddling the trout" — anyway it was a sure way of getting a feed of fish in the spring. I have often seen Indians making a rock barricade and just leaving a small opening in the rock dam, then putting a gunny-sack over this runway and then going down the stream aways and with willow sticks poking the fish upstream so they would have to end up in the gunny-sack. They sure caught a lot of fish that way while the spawning run lasted.

I kept on with my fence rail cutting for the meadow fence — each day seeing a few more done — and one evening as I was splitting some firewood outside the log cabin, getting ready to make my supper, I heard a noise and saw a young man coming towards me. He had riding britches and leggings on him, which at once told me he must be an Englishman or a land-surveyor. He was a wiry built young fellow, and of course I knew he was a stranger. Looking up at me with a half-smile on his face he said, "Are you, by any chance, called Harry Marriott?" I said, "Yes, that's me, and all that's left of him." He told me he was my cousin, Eric Collier, from Northamptonshire in faraway England, and that he had come out to British Columbia with a view to learning the cow business.

I didn't say very much, only I told him to come inside the house and we'd get supper. After we had eaten our supper and settled down to a smoke, I said to Eric, "I've little or no money to pay you or anyone else for work done, but I have lots to eat, good rough grub — beans, spuds and rice, fish and hotcakes and syrup, a couple of slices of bacon for breakfast, tea, coffee and hot biscuits." Eric listened to all this kind of careful, and said he'd like to stay and help me till he more-or-less felt his way around. I said it looked fair to me.

In early June of 1920 I was offered a job by the Ottawa government to act as a census enumerator in an area between Clinton Hill, Dog Creek and Alkali Lake Ranch and a group of settlers at Spring House Prairie a few miles above Alkali Lake. This meant that I'd have to take my team and buggy around to all the families and ranchers in that particular piece of country. The government at Ottawa wanted all the names and particulars of the ranchers, their wives and families, and a general run-down on their activities. Of course, I was sworn to secrecy in the matter, which has remained intact with me ever since.

I had some very interesting meetings with a lot of good folks I had never seen before, but knew of them, including a two-day stop-off at the famous Alkali Lake Ranch, which at that time was owned by a very fine family named Wynne-Johnson who had the respect of that whole area. They sure were real people.

I wound up my job in the Spring House area and stayed with an old-timer named Antone Boitanio and his wife and little daughter, and they certainly made me welcome in the real old-time custom. There were quite a few young people staying with the Boitanio's at that time, and they were a very friendly and musical crowd. With their fiddles, guitars and chording along on an old organ that was there, they could really roll out quite a concert. I'll tell you, it was sure a good change for me to get where there were some people, and real good meals cooked — when compared to the more-or-less work, eat and sleep at the little meadow.

One Saturday morning I was standing by the big corral at Antone Boitanio's when I saw two girls riding by the corral. One was a brown-haired gal riding a bay horse, and the other was a dark-haired gal riding a bay horse. Both of them were loping along on their horses, and I became interested as to who the brown-haired gal was. One of the boys around Spring House told me that her name was Miss Price, and that she was the school-ma'am at the Spring House school, which was a mile or two up the road. Well, it didn't take this cowboy very long before I figured I had business at the schoolhouse, and I at once began to be really interested in this smart and charming little gal.

Chapter 9

Eric Collier and My Peg

I CAME BACK DOWN to the little meadow on Big Bar Creek — after turning in all the information I had gathered to a district office at Salmon Arm, and in a little while I got a cheque for over two hundred dollars in wages for my census-taking job. I also had the address of the cute little school-ma'am and proceeded to write her as often as I could.

I bought a new mower and a hayrake with some of my census-taking money. Eric and I started in to cut and put up the wild hay that was growing in the meadow and we stacked it up for the winter use. I looked after the team and horse work, Eric did the cooking and helped pitching and together we put up around forty tons of hay, which was plenty for my little bunch of cattle and horses that winter.

In the meantime I had been keeping up an eager-beaver lot of letter-writing to my gal friend, Miss Price. When school term started around in September 1920, this young lady had applied for and got the position of school-ma'am at the 70 Mile House on the Cariboo Road. The 70 Mile House was only about twenty-two miles east of Big Bar Lake if you rode the trails and short-cuts to The Road. Every Saturday afternoon I'd get myself a shave and rummage my clothes to see if I could find some half-clean ones, and socks without a hole in them — often borrowing some of Eric's clothes if they looked better. Then I'd step up on my smart little saddle horse I called Snoozer and I'd make a bee-line to see my little school-ma'am. We'd have the weekends together, and I'd get back to the meadow at all hours on Monday mornings. The final answer to this was that a few days after Christmas 1920, Peg Price and I got married at her folks' home in Burnaby. After a few days honeymooning in Victoria, we came on up to Clinton and proceeded to the log cabin in the little meadow below the Big Bar Lake homestead.

Peg has always been a wonderful girl and a great home-maker. It was quite a change for a girl to quit teaching school and start making a home miles away from anyone, no one but me around, except for an odd rider passing through the trail. There's one sure thing about a young fellow and a girl starting out in life on a half-lonesome spot and that is, they must certain sure think a hell-rarin' pile of each other, as they are together day by day and don't see any variety much in the way of day by day living. If Peg ever felt lonesome or bored, she never complained about it. We had a few cattle then, and Peg and I fed them twice a day, and once a week we'd drive out and get our mail, which was over a twenty-five mile trip.

My cousin, Eric, left us, and started out on the long trail to Chilcotin, where he afterwards took up a large area of land around Meldrum Creek for trapline purposes. He married a very smart local girl, and they built up a trapline second to none in beavers and muskrats, Eric becoming an expert in all matters that had to do with wild life.

Peg and I lived in that comfortable log cabin just as snug as two bugs in a rug. We went to Clinton in the spring and in the fall with the team and a road-wagon buggy which held a lot of grub. It was quite an event. We'd stay at the old Clinton Hotel overnight and enjoy the luxury of a hot bath in which you could stretch out, instead of bathing in the old round tin tub — half in, half out sort of game, and all humped up like a constipated crane — which we had to do at home.

I had a kind of a rough, but an odd, trip in late March of 1922. I knew the snow was starting to go, so I thought I'd do better to ride a saddle horse down to Jesmond, about fourteen miles away from the meadow, and get our mail at the post office there. When I got there at about three in the afternoon of mail day, I found that my friend, Harry Coldwell, had not arrived with the mail from Clinton, so I stayed on expecting him to come along any minute. Time kept sliding along, and I could see Mrs. Coldwell was getting real worried, so about 7 o'clock I told her I'd better start out looking for him in case he had got into a jackpot along the road, and was in trouble.

I started out on the road, and it was sure slow going mile after mile, the snow real soft and deep and mushy. Every step my horse took he went down the soft snow to the road bottom, and after riding this way for nine miles I came on Harry Coldwell driving along at a snail's pace. It appears he had broken his double-trees that the team pulled on, and he'd had to take his jack-knife and whittle himself out another double-tree from a jack-pine pole.

Well, we got back to Jesmond around one the next morning. I gave my horse a good rest and got a bite to eat and some strong coffee, and I started back the fourteen miles to the meadow. The moon was trying to break through the cloudy sky as I rode on home, and my horse was getting tired from miles of weaving through the deep soft snow, and when I got within about six miles from home I heard the most weird cry coming from somewhere in the timber to the right of the trail. It sounded to me like some woman, or maybe a kid screaming — and I stopped and listened. The piercing scream let out once more, so I turned my horse into the timber and hollered out, "Where are you? I'm coming." There was no answer so, very much puzzled, I wheeled back for the trail and listened for a few minutes more. Then I figured I'd better keep on going.

When I got home I found Peg in bed and very nervous, wondering if anything had happened to me, so I told her the story and fell fast asleep. I'd had one hell of a trip. Next day I meditated all day, turning over in my old bean what could have made such a wild scream like someone in pain, away out in that timber with no one around for miles that I knew of. A few days later a friend of mine, called Gussie Haller, came riding through there and I told him about this strange wild noise I had heard down the trail. He said it must have been a cougar screaming and crying. Well, I'd never seen or heard a cougar in action before, and I've never heard one since, but I'll sure say it gave me quite a start at that.

Well, such is life in these thin settled ranges and you have to try and be ready for anything that comes along, and do your best to battle any of these sudden upsets when you run into them.

Gussie Haller was a son of the old pioneer, Joe Haller, and a brother to Eddie who had gone overseas with us in that World War mix-up — and if there ever was a real man on a horse, it was Gussie. His main interest in life was to run and catch wild horses, and in those years they were thicker than fiddlers in Hell on the Big Bar ranges. Most of them unbranded and Gussie caught a lot of them. Sometimes by running them down on a good grain-fed horse and roping them and breaking them to lead right then and there. At other times he'd put up a corral out of jack-pine logs, a round corral always — because you sure don't want to have any corners in a corral, otherwise you could get maybe in a jack-pot if you had a wild horse, or even a wild cow can get you kind of foul in a corner. Sometimes for a two or three hundred yard stretch he'd run long wings out, made out of rails so as the wild horses would have to follow the wings down, the first thing you know they'd come down to the opening or mouth of the corral and, believe me, you'd have to be right at their tails and get the gate closed or corral bars up, otherwise they'd turn and head out right on top of you. The corral has to be high, and pretty solid because these wild cayuses could sure jump high when cornered up.

Sometimes Gussie would get another rider to help him — one riding around and starting the bunch in the direction of the corral and the other rider keeping out of sight as much as he could, and when the bunch came to the wings, he'd haze them on down to the corral and get the bars up. It was real dangerous work, but a very exciting, sporty job, and out-smarting those wild cayuses was a real challenge to any man's ability on a horse. It took quite a man, and a real horse, to cut through the timber and keep up to a bunch of wild horses running through the bush. There was never enough money in that game to equal up the work of making wild horse corrals, getting a whole pile of bruises, skinned shin-bones and shoulders from tearing along through those rocks and brush, but Gussie loved the game and he was sure good at it.

The best time to get these wild cayuses was just before the snow melted in the last part of March, as they were mostly thin and could not run as well after having to paw snow and eat frozen grass all winter. In after years the government shot a lot of them.

These wild cayuses made tough, hardy saddle horses when caught and broke to ride, but most of them never forgot their early days as a wild horse, and if ever they were turned loose in a pasture they were generally always ready to run like hell before being caught.

I owned one years ago, and in two years I just caught him twice and rode him. It took me quite a ride to catch him each time, even in a fair-sized pasture, so I figured wild-horse running was a crazy game. All you got out of it was to run a good horse to death just to catch a real nuisance, because if you turned him loose you just had got yourself another job to catch him again. I have gentled them down from running in a pasture by tieing a short piece of chain about two feet long around an ankle on a front foot so when they run the chain would bang them around on their feet and legs, which would surely slow them up. Putting hobbles on their front feet was not too good, because when they caught onto it, they could run just the same for quite aways. I have sometimes hobbled them — one front foot to a hind foot — which is kind of rough on them, but if you have to have a horse to ride, anything beats going afoot.

We plugged along in the summer of 1922, and put up our little stacks of hay in the meadow, riding together, looking after our little bunch of heifers, and Old Man Winter came along. We fed the cattle good, and were warm and comfortable in the log house, with lots of grub, firewood, and always the creek handy for water. I had nearly all the meadow fenced now, and felt right along that we were making some headway.

In the winter of 1923, along about the first week in February, we got quite a rough jolt as I got a notice from the Government Agent at Clinton telling me, in cold official language, that I must actually go and live on the Big Bar Lake homestead, and giving me thirty days to get living on it again, or it would be cancelled. I had already lived in the lake homestead cabin for the best part of a year and a half and had fenced it, and done other improvements, and was on the place at least three times a week. It was quite a shock to have to move house and home in winter months. However, I made up my mind that I would not lose the work and efforts I had done at the lake homestead.

Bit by bit, Peg and I loaded up our stoves, beds and furniture and belongings on a sleigh — one load every day, and often a lot of heavy lifting for Peg — so finally we got moved up to the lake. Our cabin at the lake was not nearly as comfortable or fixed up as well as the log house at the meadow, but Peg was the kind of girl — and is today — that things have to be awful rough before she starts crying or complaining, so with a few rolls of heavy white building paper and some tacks, me helping out all I could, we tried to get things a little more like home.

I sure had little use for that particular Government Agent in Clinton. He was a short pint-sized Englishman that figured he knew it all, and his head was so full he couldn't even take another spoonful of know-how in his head. Just rule-of-thumb product of hidebound bureaucracy — he would have starved to death if he'd ever have had to make a living at anything else. While there are good and bad in all people and nations, it seemed to me that a real snotty-nosed poop like him was a poor character to have in that sort of job, which required some agreeable personality, tact and human nature knowledge. This fellow would not agree to me moving back a little later when the weather warmed up, instead of snow and sub-zero weather to move out in. However, we made it. The snow got soft and melted in the spring, the ice in the lake went away, and the creek boomed along, rushing to the Fraser.

The lake was always a deep blue colour, especially in the centre of the lake. It was about two and a half miles long, and maybe about seven hundred yards at its widest point. It was plumb full of native fish called Kamloops trout, running from ¾ of a pound to two pounds in weight — a very game fighting type of fish. The species are still there in reasonable quantity, but many changes have taken place at the lake since those years.

The name of Big Bar got its origin from a big gravel bar in the Fraser River just above the spot where Big Bar Creek runs into the river. The creek is about twenty-eight miles long and runs through two lakes. The uppermost lake was called Big Bar Lake, and the smaller lake, which was several miles or more down the creek from Big Bar Lake, was called the Little Bar Lake.

I just don't know of any place more peaceful looking and down to old Mother Earth, than Big Bar Lake is, particularly in the early spring and summer. I liked to sit down on the sidehill above the lake in the early morning, hearing the meadow-larks singing their spring song, the squirrels cheeping away with their everlasting chatter, the low quacking of a mother duck teaching her little brood to swim, the plaintive and lonesome cry of the loons on the lake, the wof-wof-wof sharp bark of a coyote tirelessly trotting along in search of something to eat, and then getting disgusted, sitting on his tailbone howling — and maybe getting an answering howl from his mate.

All these things bring a very sober and reflecting thought to my mind — that I, and all human beings, are just a very small cog in the great machine created by the All Powerful Creator.

In the end of that year I rustled around and cut myself a set of jack-pine logs for a barn and a new corral at the lake. I always peeled the bark off the logs, because when the logs dry out they sure last for a long time, and a peeled log is not nearly as attractive to a wandering bug, as one with the bark left on.

I was kind of pleased that I had become a good wood-butcher with an axe, and I was well able to lay up logs for a barn or a house without having big cracks between the logs. There is nothing worse, or more greenhorn work, than to have so many big cracks in between the cabin logs that anyone could see you sitting at the table by just looking through the big cracks as he rode along. You can always tell by looking at the corners of a log cabin wall whether a man knows anything about the game of logwork or not. It has almost become a gone and forgotten art in these days of plywood and other new-fangled methods of house building. But those days a fellow with an axe and a short-blade crosscut-saw — and probably a hunk of chewing tobacco — could really go to putting up a cabin.

We carried along, and had many serious hard times those years especially in the line of getting any cash income from the ranch and a small bunch of cattle. Our little income was greatly helped by me and my team getting a month or so's work from the Public Works

Department of our district. The job called for clearing windfalls, taking out rocks, and cutting brush on the road which ran on the south side of Big Bar Lake down to the settlement away down on Big Bar Creek.

The problem of making a living and making it stick, building up a small ranch with little or no cash, all-in-all confronted us with a lot of difficult and hard times in terms of money. We always had plenty to eat, and clothes to wear — although my clothes didn't go beyond overalls and workshirts, with Stanfield's woollen underwear — the best ever. I had one good suit of clothes which I'd wear once a year, on Christmas Day.

In the late fall of 1923, Peg started to get some real pain in her right side and it began to worry us both considerable. It happened that one evening our old friend, Father Thomas of the Catholic Mission near the 150 Mile House, called in on us and stayed overnight. Although the grand old priest and I were not of the same religious ideas, we sure were great friends just the same. I respected and admired that fine old Frenchman who had given his whole life to the Indians and settlers in our far-spread-out Cariboo. Everybody loved old Father Thomas, and if the folks of his flock would not live as he tried to tell them, it sure did not hurt them any to listen to him anyway.

Peg and I both told the Father about the pain that was continually bothering her, and he told me that he was only an amateur doctor but he felt sure Peg had appendicitis, and I'd better get her out to a hospital as quick as I could. Next day I drove Peg up to our nearest neighbours, the Ike Kerr family, who lived about fifteen miles away and only four miles from the Cariboo Road. They were longtime friends of ours all through the years, and first-class neighbours.

They had an old-time Model T Ford car, which was a real top-hand outfit at that time, and he drove Peg down to Ashcroft, where she took the C.P.R. train to Vancouver. I knew she'd get to her ma and dad, and the doctor, and a hospital, so I returned to the lake anxious, and doing a whole hell of a pile of worrying, just in case things did not turn out right.

About two days later I stepped up on my Snoozer horse and rode up to Kerr's. He always brought my mail from Clinton as far as their ranch — and sure enough I had a wire from Peg's dad telling me Peg had been operated on and could I come down? So, with a kind of nervous feeling I struck out for Vancouver and headed for St. Paul's Hospital where I saw Peg. She was quite weak but recovering, so I stayed in Burnaby with her folks for several days, going to the hospital every day. When they told me she was out of danger I started back to the lake. After a while Peg came back, and how glad I was to have her home again.

Sickness and accidents were always a serious problem to run into in the backwoods range country, because it's a long way to get any kind of medical help, and doctor's bills and expenses really rolled up into a hell of a big bill, which would mean that a fellow would be on the old grindstone working to pay them off for a mighty long spell. In those years, an average fellow was darn near down-and-out before he headed out to see a pill-shooter, and, of course, in many cases the settler let it go far too late to be much use. With better roads and some sort of a car or truck to get out with, it has become easier to get any doctoring looked at, but even in this day and age, the nearest hospital is at Ashcroft, fifty-seven miles away, and in this isolated area, and in thinly-settled places, it will probably never be much different.

The following year of 1924 saw us getting more and more looking like a little ranch ought to be, with a snug little barn, corral, a tool-shed, a chicken-house with a couple dozen hens, our own little bunch of cattle up to around forty-odd head, a couple of good milk cows, a work team and three good saddle horses, a real good set of haying machines, but darn little ready cash of any kind. That summer I ploughed up around twenty-two acres, and figured on putting in some fall rye which I could cut for hay the following summer. At the same time I applied for the Crown Grant, or title-deed from the government in Victoria. In due time the government homestead inspector came along to size up the improvements. His name was Tommy Dougherty, a brother of Charlie Dougherty at the 23 Mile Ranch below Clinton, and after quite a lot of argument back and forth, he agreed to recommend to the government that the title-deed be granted.

The homestead at the lake was the first and last time I ever took on a homesteading deal, because the land could be bought from the

Land Department on terms of payment, which made it better all around, as against the method of homesteading it, but you had to be more-or-less a bona fide resident to qualify for purchase.

In July of 1925 our son Ronnie was born in Vancouver, and a few weeks later I went down there on a flying trip and brought Peg and the baby home to the Lake, and I was pleased and proud of both of them.

Towards October of 1925 I had a pretty good offer from the B.C. Cattle Co. at Canoe Creek Ranch where I had been foreman for six months in 1919. Peg and I did quite a lot of meditating — I was to be the foreman and have charge of the ranch work, and Peg was to look after the big ranch house and attend to the store which had all Indian customers — mostly from the reserve at Canoe Creek. We accepted this offer and I sold my little bunch of cattle and rented my little meadow and the lake homestead to a local man called Philip Boston. On the first day of October, Peg and I, and our baby, Ronnie, arrived at Canoe Creek Ranch.

The ranch manager at that time was a tall rangy man named Lincoln Calhoun Hannon, who had come from Texas into British Columbia about twenty years earlier. I had known Linc Hannon for around twelve years or more, and he being of an age where he could not stand the heavy day-to-day round of work and riding, the company at Victoria, B.C., had given him permission to load a lot of his responsibility to a younger man's shoulders, and the young man was myself.

Hannon was a real capable ranch manager and very little ever got by his attention. He was a number one cattleman, and could size up a bunch of cattle better than most ranchers I knew in that area. Neat and tidy, the ranch buildings and fences were always kept up in good shape. He spoke with that Southern Texas drawl, always more-or-less a silent type of fellow — but once in a while he'd break loose and tell me of his boyhood days in Texas. It sure was interesting to hear him tell of some of those well-known characters of the south, and the early cattle drives from Texas as far north as the State of Montana.

Chapter 10

Round-Ups and Drives
Canoe Creek Ranch

I FELL INTO the normal swing of the Canoe Creek Ranch at once and looked after all the practical details of the outfit under Mr. Hannon's orders — and I had a very busy job. A ranch of that size called for a very steady diet of everyday work, long hours, and many Sundays included, but it was something I liked doing, and the cow work just suited me to a queen's taste, because in those days I was rated as a real good man around cattle. There is an awful big difference in the ways of handling twelve hundred head of cattle, and looking after them, than there is in just working on a small ranch set-up.

The ranch put up about seven hundred tons of alfalfa in the two crops each year, and branded around three hundred and twenty calves every summer. I'd take out about seven Indians at the end of June and we'd be gone for about eight days or so rounding up the calves — branding the calves with a ▲ (triangle) brand on the right hip, and cutting their right ear off close and cutting a small dewlap on their brisket. Wrestling to throw calves down on their left sides for branding and castrating was a lot of fun for the Indian boys — they most often made a lot of extra heavy effort for themselves, but they sure enjoyed it.

After the hay was all up I'd take out the boys again, and we'd round up the beef, and bring in the bulls, and the cows and calves for weaning. The calves would have to be kept in a real well-fenced yard for about a week at weaning time, because their ma's would never leave for several days. It is a rough time for the calves because they get cut off from ma's milk and loving, and sometimes work up quite a temperature from excitement and continual bawling, and the ma's used to be bothered with a certain amount of fever in their bags too.

Conditions change as years go by and now calves are vaccinated against haemorrhagic septicemia commonly known as cattle-flu, to which calves are subject at weaning time. Nowadays, I know of cow outfits that corral their cows and calves right on the range and truck the calves home — two to twenty miles — where they can't see or hear their ma's, which is a much more satisfactory deal all around.

Mr. Hannon always went to the coast for the winter when I was there and I had to look after the outfit, Peg and I by ourselves with one or two men. I didn't feed over one-third of the Canoe Creek cattle herd the winters I was there. Just the calves, the bulls and some thin cows if there were any. The rest of them ran out on their twenty miles of winter range, and several times a week I was riding among them — gathering up a few poor cows if I saw they were falling off and needing feeding some hay to, and I'll sure say that old Canoe Creek was a real economical spread to run.

Hannon was real good in case of emergency — in his frontier-trained style. I remember having a crew at China Gulch, one of the outside camps, where I was putting up a new fence, about five miles long, for the ranch. I had a young Indian boy on the crew, and he became very much bound up after filling up on a lot of good plain grub in the first few days he came to work there. The young fellow was in a lot of pain, and I had no salts or medicine of any kind in the camp. As luck would have it, Hannon came riding along over the mountain to take a looksee how I was making out with the new fence, so I told him about this Indian boy, and the pain he was in — sometimes rolling on the ground and holding his belly with his hands, groaning with pain. At dinner time we all went to the China Gulch cabin to eat and after dinner Hannon saw an old rusty button-hook which belonged to old Mathilda, the camp cook, so he took the button-hook and warmed it up and greased it with some hot beef tallow in a tin saucer on the stove, and then I and an Indian held the Indian boy down on an old wooden bunk while Hannon gave the boy a very thorough and real smart enema with this tallow-greased button-hook — which produced a great result from the Indian boy. Years after when the boy had grown to be a man, every time I saw him, I'd remember Hannon and his bunch-grass doctoring that saved this boy's life.

It was after this some months, when an old Indian showed me a low-branched little bush, which we know as a hooshem-berry bush — it has little red berries on it and is fairly common on all the high ranges. Well, old Dick Jim, the Indian, told me that if ever I got bound up bad, if I took some of the roots of this hooshem-berry bush and boiled them in some water, and drank the tea from it, it would sure help out pretty quick. Some years after, I tried it out on one occasion and all I can say to anyone who wants to try it in an emergency is, you'd better be undoing your pants buttons the minute you take the cup in your hand, or you may find yourself in trouble.

My days were always filled up — busier than a one-armed paper-hanger with the hives — around that old ranch. Peg looked after the house and the store which supplied a lot of the grub and clothes that the Indians needed most. The prices to them were very high. The Indian, on the whole, is a very stoical and uncomplaining sort of fellow and he always takes a long time to consider and reconsider before he buys anything. No one must ever be in a hurry if he is trying to sell things to an Indian, and in most cases he has always been the easy mark for the quick-thinking white trader. In my time I've seen brass brooches sold for two dollars and a half that were only worth fifteen cents in a store in Kamloops — but an Indian loves colours and if he wanted to wear that piece of phoney jewelry on his coat, or on his hat, or if he wanted a real fancy-coloured shirt, he bought it — regardless.

Each year at Canoe Creek we had about a four days' beef drive to take the beef out to the P.G.E. railroad at Chasm — or the 59 Mile as it was called. October was the usual month of shipment, and this was followed by a smaller drive in December.

We used to drive around two hundred and fifty head in the October drive, which was ten carloads each year when I was there. Mostly the fat two- and three-year-old steers, some heifers and fat dry cows. As a rule if a cow did not have a calf in the spring or summer she was shipped for beef that fall, because no rancher can afford to feed one cow through two winters just to get one calf.

On those round-up trips, and on the beef drives, we'd take a light wagon and team for our grub and blankets, and sleep in a tent. The cook always slept just inside the tent, where it would be close and handy to get up first and get the breakfast going in the morning. The cook's job was the cooking and driving the team ahead with the wagon to the next camping spot, where, when we came along with the drive that evening, the camp and tent would be all set up, and supper ready. Sometimes we'd have to night herd, and take it in turns to ride herd through the night. You'd never have much trouble after the cattle laid down, for as a rule if the cattle are laying down at dark, they won't move around much till daylight. This was a real good life, and I sure loved it, and used to look forward to the beef drives.

I was always a cautious boy when we were sleeping in a tent, to make sure that my little bedroll did not actually touch the Indian cowboys blankets as those fellows had all got lice of sorts and sizes. The snoring and scratching that went on in the tent every night would have done credit to any Italian musical opera. I surely was as careful as I could be, so as not to bring any of this galloping dandruff into the Canoe Creek house and to Peg and little Ronnie. However, in these last years the coming of D.D.T. and other bug killers have nowadays changed the picture entirely. I have a great old side-kicker of mine who I always call Uncle Bill (whom I will mention later in my story) but he had a remedy for getting rid of lice whenever he ran into a batch. He told me quite seriously that he sprinkled some snoose — which is the loggers' brand of snuff — right around the edges of his shirt collar, and the seams of his long Stanfield woollen underwear, and whenever a louse came in contact with the snoose he just naturally sneezed himself to death.

In the early spring of 1927 I got a chance to buy another little hay meadow about thirteen miles towards Clinton from the lake homestead. It had a nice little house on it, a good barn and about 75 tons of hay on it every year. I rustled up enough money to put down the first payment on it, and the owner gave me several years before I had to pay any more, so it looked like a pretty fair deal to me.

Under the circumstances Peg and I figured we'd better leave our job at the Canoe Creek Ranch, as we had now increased the spread quite a bit. We had both of us saved our wages at Canoe Creek, so we had a little ready cash to help out again. We moved up to our new addition, which Peg named Pine Crest as it gave a very clear view of the mountains running from Clinton to Big Bar Lake.

In the fall of 1927 the Canoe Creek Ranch was purchased by Mr. Henry Koster, my old neighbour from the Crow's Bar-Gang Ranch days, and it is still in the hands of the Koster family today, and they surely do own a real good ranch. In the summer of that year, I agreed to get the hay at Pine Crest put up on a 50-50 share basis, and I got an Indian friend of mine to put up the wild hay down at the little meadow for around six dollars a ton put in the stack.

Peg had saved up some money while she was at Canoe Creek Ranch with me, and she needed a little holiday, so she and little Ronnie went down and stayed with her folks in Burnaby for about a month or so. I was always out to pick up any ready cash to help out our income, and so I was offered a job for myself and team and light wagon for a month. The job being to cook for, and move camp around, where needed for a government surveyor friend of mine, named Captain Geoffrey Downton. His very capable brain and powers of observation made possible the huge power development in the Bridge River area in later years. I certainly enjoyed that month or so, cooking and camp tending for this real top-hand gentleman and surveyor, and his chain-man, Roy Birkholder, of the Lillooet country, and as I knew the area from the 57 Mile Creek to the head-waters of Canoe Creek very well, I was able to give my surveyor boss a whole pile of useful information which I think was of real help to him in his reports to Victoria.

Around September of that year there came a vacancy for a part-time job as a deputy Provincial Brand Inspector for the Clinton, Chasm and Lone Butte areas, along the P.G.E. railroad, and in due time I got the job. It called for a lot of careful looking at brands, and being real sure that the cattle were branded with the ranchers' and shippers' brand, and keeping records of days, dates, and numbers of cattle sold, and the meat-packing concerns that bought them. Each month I'd have to send in the report to the Recorder of Brands at Victoria.

I had a lot of long saddle horse rides to make on the inspection trips and I'd get back to Pine Crest, or to the Lake generally pretty late in the evening, having been away all day from early morning. I got $5.00 a day wages from the government, for every inspection trip, and that bit of cash really helped to keep the mulligan-pot on the stove with something to eat in it.

I had very little trouble in my years as a brand inspector with regard to anyone trying to steal cattle. A stockyard is not a good setting for a cow thief to operate in. The most careful time of the year would be from late November on, when the cattle started to get their winter hair. However, I always had a lasso rope and a pair of clippers, and I could throw a critter down and stretch him out if necessary, and go to clipping him, or corner him up in some chute if I was uncertain of the brand. My experience as regards cow stealing has been kind of limited, as I was never in that business, and while I have been certain sure myself that some of it went on in the range areas, I was never able to bring the hundred per cent proof of it, which a court of law would require. As I have known it, it resolves itself into two kinds of cow stealing — stealing unbranded calves, or butchering a calf or yearling for meat. I have known of one old fellow who used to ride out with a sack behind his saddle and pick up a young calf just a few days old, put it in the sack behind his saddle and head for home and put the calf as an extra on his gentle milk cow. Others would probably shoot the cow down in a timber patch, and a day or so later come and drive the slick calf home and brand it. There were a few more odd ways of getting the slick-ears but it's not much use trying to steal a calf if his ma is around, as she will always be hanging around not too far from the last place she saw her calf. If the ranch is at all isolated the better chance the cow thief has to operate. With regards to the butchering on the range, it was a limited sort of game. Where a ranch is located reasonably, next and nigh to small settlers and nesters, as we call the homesteaders, there is always the chance that a fat range calf — which would weigh around two hundred pounds dressed out, with the guts, hide, feet and head off — would be more than welcome in a settler's cabin, and that amount of meat could easily be used up by a family and maybe some of their friends.

It's a sure certain thing that any of this range butchering is done before sunrise an hour or two, or else just before sundown, and the only place for that is in the timber, and pack the meat out on a gentle pack horse, in sacks. Anyone in this little game has got to be a night or real early morning rider, and he's got to know enough to keep off trails and government roads where he could leave tracks, and he's got to try and get rid of the hide somehow — either by burying it or piling brush on it. The calf's ma would probably be bawling around not too far away from where he'd butchered the calf, and she'd hang around for four or five days before she'd give up and go away. Of course, butchering a yearling would not be so much trouble, but there would be the problem of having more meat.

I never caught anyone butchering on the range, but I am sure it had been done, in cases where a small settler with a lot of kids to feed, just had to have some kind of meat. I know of one old Indian with eight or ten kids who I know darned well never fed the kids bacon. He told me that he'd got so he could not eat veal without it making him vomit, and I figured it out myself that he'd eat so many of my friends' calves that his belly coudn't stand the gaff any more.

I have always told the government tyees that it was far better to let these settlers shoot their deer, moose or birds, and catch fish, in or out of season, because if these settlers and Indians could not get any game or meat they would eat the cattlemen's calves or yearlings, legal or illegal, before they would go hungry. These folks can't afford any kind of high-tone grub like premium bacon or canned sausages.

Cow stealing in most any kind of form don't pay in the final adding up of the score, because some day the cow thief will get careless maybe, and get caught out. Then whether he is proved guilty or not guilty, the lawyer man rolls up a big bill agin him, to defend him in court, so it all comes to a real high-priced deal.

In the days I speak of, there were no government cheques for a man with a bunch of kids — but times have changed for the better, and the rough struggle for survival is nothing nowadays when you compare it with forty years ago.

Every range country I have ever known or heard of in my long years has been touched up a little with this calf stealing and calf butchering game, all the way from Texas to Canada, particularly where ranches were operating nearby to settlers. The only thing a rancher could do would be to ride out on his range on a good horse, and poke around his cattle as often as he could — which is a real necessary thing in ranch operating.

The winter of 1927 came around and saw Peg and I and little Ronnie all pretty snug up at Pine Crest. We had around seventy head of cattle, and, of course, some debt against our layout, but I was really rustling along and doing my damndest to keep any possible wolf away from the door. That winter I fed our cattle, and between times I'd cut jack-pine firewood with an axe and a crosscut-saw. I'd haul one or two loads into Clinton, which was eleven miles away, with my team and sleigh every week, and the wood money would be used up for buying grub in the store. Between cutting firewood and my part-time brand inspecting job, and my little bunch of cows, I figured I stood a chance of finally getting somewhere, maybe — but I never allowed myself any ideas of not making it because nothing is ever gained or made unless you have some get-up and rustle about yourself.

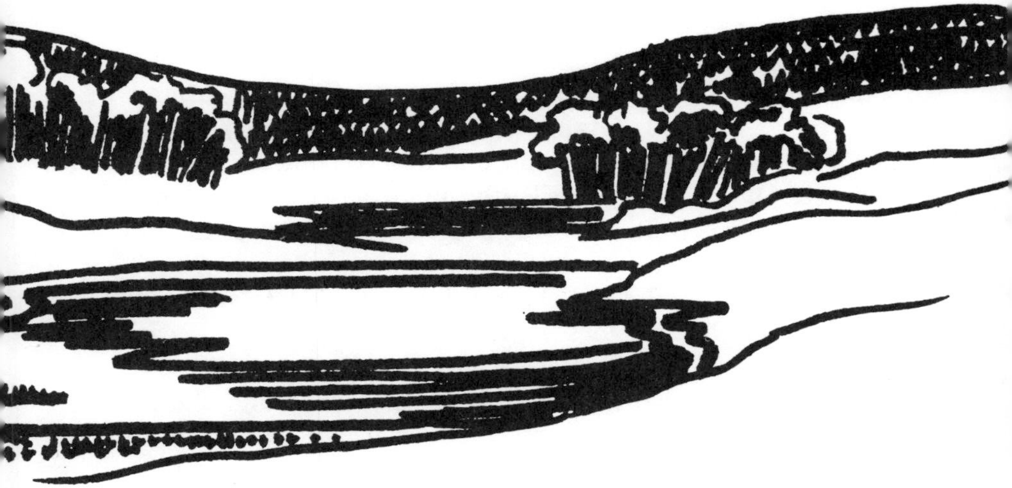

Chapter 11

Peg's Guest Ranch Foxes Depression

THE LONG WINTER finally petered out, and signs of spring started to show up in the latter end of March 1928. The first signs, most general, were the arrival of two or three crows flying around, followed by others a little later. The warm wind swept up from the Thompson River Valley, which was south of our Pine Crest, loosening up the snow, and starting to melt it. My cows were real heavy in calf, and I'd sure be feeding them good so as they could stand the heavy strain in the last month or so before they calved — all the hay they could eat and clean up every day, because the cow is first and last the most important item on any man's ranch. They are, by-and-large, his meal ticket, and no one but a fool will be careless with that, no matter what kind of a game he is in.

One day in the last few days in March, I was outside the house at Pine Crest, right after noon, sawing some firewood, when I heard a sound of a saddle horse's feet on the road. Turning around I saw it was my old friend, Grandad Bishop, from the 57 Mile Ranch and I said "Howdy" to him and told him to come in and get a bite of dinner. Old Jim Bishop silently handed me an envelope and it was a cablegram from far-away England telling me that my dear old mother had gone over the "High Mountain" and was resting in the arms of the good Lord. I sure did feel her loss very badly, for while I never did get to see her more than on two occasions in twenty years, yet I always wrote letters to her once a week — and never missed over two weeks in all those years — and she done the same for me. But time is a great healer. Death comes to all of us and when the good Lord names our day it won't matter how many smart doctors you've got waiting on you, you are going to go anyhow, and the guy with a million bucks, his head ain't going to be any higher in the air than a poor old Indian's when that time drifts along.

In the early part of May I had turned quite a few cows out on the range, and late one Saturday afternoon I figured I'd ride down to the lake and see what the cattle were doing. So I climbed on Nellie, a real good cow-mare, and struck out for Big Bar Lake. Along about six that evening I rode up on top of a big high knoll at the east end of the lake, and looking around, I thought I could see a cow bogged down in the mud on the edge of the lake. I turned down off the knoll and loped up to where I saw the cow, and sure enough it was my cow all right. Before I got through looking around I found three more of my cows stuck tighter than hell in this mud, and all of them dead. I stayed at the cabin that night and early next morning I drove all the cattle I could find away from the lake and that mud. From that day to this I have always tried to watch out for that treacherous strip of a muddy bog — especially in the spring, when cattle are always a little bit on the weak side. These ups and downs happen to each and all of us in the game of life, and we have to learn to take them in our stride, always hoping and praying that there won't be more downs than ups as continual runs of downs will put any of us walking the road afoot, and talking to ourselves.

I had a very busy summer and put up quite a little bit of hay that year, and together with my little cash income from the odd government job with me and my team, and the brand inspecting job every so often, I was starting to make things look like I was really in business. That year, towards fall, I bought the smartest little cow-horse I ever owned, for forty dollars, from a nephew of my old friends, Eddie and Gussie Haller of Big Bar.

I called this little bay horse Sunny Jim, and he was all horse, believe me. Tougher than whalebone, he could turn on a nickel, and every so often he'd take a notion to buck, or he'd jump straight up in the air and fall over backwards. This last stunt he'd have of raring up and coming over backwards kind of scared me a little, as very often a horse falling over backwards can get a fellow in a real foul jackpot. So after a bit of meditating on how to cure him of this raring up and falling backwards game, I figured I'd ride him with a fairly loose cinch on the saddle, and a lot of slack in my bridle lines, and so in time I got Sunny Jim to forget his dangerous little trick, and I had many years of real faithful rides from old Sunny.

I had my brother-in-law and his wife, Bill and Grace Price, up on the ranch that summer, and I have never had a better worker than Bill Price. Towards the late fall Bill wanted to go hunting on the mountain and see if he could shoot a moose, so he and a good local boy called Isadore Grinder, tied some grub on behind their saddles and rode off into the high rugged rock country behind Pine Crest, up on the mountain.

A day and a half later I saw him riding down the trail with something tied in a blood-stained sack. I thought he and Isadore had got their moose for sure — so when he rode up to the bars I said to him, "Well, Bill, I guess you were kind of lucky, eh?" Bill only grunted, and said he had some meat. Anyway, I took and hung this part of a hindquarter up, in the little log milk-house with the creek running right through it, and cut off two or three steaks. At supper time Peg had these steaks fried just right, with lots of good gravy and French fried spuds, and we all thought it was fine, and too bad we didn't have a lot more of it. We invited up the local Anglican preacher and his wife from Clinton, and the postmaster from there with his wife also, and all and sundry figured they'd had a real good Sunday dinner, and were real loud in their praise of moose meat, and of Peg's top-hand cooking. About four or five days after this, I went down one morning to cut off a roast and there was sure a strong smell coming off the meat, and I figured it was starting to get bad, so I took and threw it away in the willow brush below the house, kind of disgusted that it had started to spoil that quick.

It was two months or more after this, and Bill and his missus had gone back to the coast, that Isadore was helping me for a day at Pine Crest and he told me, with a big grin on his face, that when he and Bill had camped out on the mountain hunting moose, they could find nothing but tracks, and tracks always make poor soup, so before they would allow they were skunked on their trip, they shot a two-year-old filly, an unbranded little sorrel mare. They took the best part of each hindquarter and brought them into camp, Bill bringing his chunk of horse meat down to Pine Crest with him. I've eaten a lot of moose meat since, but at that time I guess I didn't know the difference either, as I'd never eaten any horse meat before. I tried many times afterwards to get Bill to admit it was horse meat he'd brought in, but I never got a "yes" or a "no" out of him.

I had another kind of important event that fall. When I was in Clinton one day a friend of mine said to me, "Why don't you get holt of a little car of some kind or other, Harry?" I told him I'd never given the matter a lot of thought. He went on to tell me about a pretty fair Ford Model T. It was a second-hand one but had not racked up too many miles, and I could get it for one hundred dollars.

So I bought this Model T Ford for the hundred dollars and the garage man in Clinton, named Gilmore Olsen, gave me several lessons, so I started to learn. Of course I made quite a few errors on the start, especially in stopping the darned thing, and had a habit of hollering "Whoa!" when I wanted to stop, but as time went on I got so that I could drive pretty fair, and Peg and I and Ronnie used to drive to Clinton to get our mail and groceries every week. Sometimes some of the boys around Clinton would josh me and say, "Harry, why don't you get yourself a good car instead of this old rattle-trap?" I'd come back at them with this one, "If your hind-end had been bumped and calloused up for as many years as mine has, sitting on a saddle horse for mile after mile, this old car seat would feel pretty good to you at that." That was not stretching the truth for sure.

However, it didn't take me too long to find out that riding along in comfort on the seat of a car was a whole pile more expensive than riding a saddle horse because the gas fumes rolling away from the back end of the car all meant it cost money, and plenty of it. The saddle horse just cost you some grass and hay, and you were raising that anyhow. The car would get you there, and probably bring you back again, in away less time than jogging along on a cayuse at around five miles an hour, although I'll sure always believe the saddle horse is the most dependable, as mud-holes, ice or snow mean very little to him. You'll always get there, and that doesn't hold good for a car a whole lot of times.

However, around that time on the Cariboo Road we were just about ready to enter into the gas and oil years which have kept on going to a point nowadays when work teams are a thing of the past. As long as our western country lasts and range folks still run cattle for a living, there will always be need for a saddle horse and a rider to sit in the middle of him, because no gas and oil rigging will ever bring the cattle in from the mountains, and the sidehills of a range country. It just can't be done yet, so the chances are real big that the cowboys and their cayuses will still be here until the good Lord rings His big gong calling everyone of us into camp.

Winter time came poking along, and saw us still making a little headway on the ranch. I put up a woodshed addition to the house at Pine Crest, and we were well stocked up for grub, clothes and hay for that winter. The spring of 1929 saw us all raring to get busy and get more done.

After I had the cattle turned out and the hay fields looked over good, I got a job. Me and my team, together with the Kerr boys and their outfit, made six miles of road for the government. We cleared a whole pile of jack-pine out, and made a passable road out of what had once been a cow trail. This six miles of road was running from Big Bar Lake eastward to the 59 Mile Creek, and by that we made the distance to Clinton four or five miles shorter, so we had only twenty-four miles from the lake, which meant less time and gas and oil expense. We did a good job, and it still stands up good today.

I had a real good crop of hay that summer of 1929 and the beef cattle that I sold were in real good top shape. I sold them to the packers around the middle of September. That was a real blessing to us as along towards the end of that month, the stock-markets of New York and other money centres collapsed and went atumbling down to the ground, and the whole American country and other parts of the world, were all shattered down to the grass roots and the Great Depression was on.

Industry, wages and jobs, cattle and beef prices to the producers and ranch owners all skidded down to almost nothing, and the whole set-up became a hopeless outlook. We heard tales of long strings of folks in towns and cities lining up to be fed hot mulligan stews from the government stew kitchens — thousands broke and homeless with no jobs. Only the upper ten bracket were able to survive this economic typhoon. It was a terrible state of affairs, to see a great country like our America reach a condition where a rancher or farmer had to give his product away for little or nothing because the city dweller had no money to buy anything with.

We sold good fat cows for fifteen dollars a head, and good fat steers for around twenty to twenty-five dollars a head. In the winter of 1929 I had a pretty solid-built young fellow, named Fred Peters, cut jack-pine logs every day and all day long for fifteen dollars a month and his board, and he was mighty glad to have a home, a job and a few dollars at that.

In the fall of 1930 I came home from shipping my carload of beef cattle with a little baby cheque of $531.45 for the whole twenty-five head, which was our whole year's output. The day the beef were shipped each year was looked forward to by all ranchers and cattlemen as being one of the most particular days of the year. That was the only pay day we had in a whole year that amounted to anything.

In those depression years it became just a day of gloom and disappointment, because we knew that the whole beef cheque would only pay part of our yearly expenses and debts, and that most of us were being further bogged down in the economic pot-hole. The buyers for the meat packing companies took full advantage of the hard time situation amongst the cattlemen, knowing full well that the rancher simply had to sell his catttle. They were a perishable product and could be held over only so long. The real rugged deals handed out to some of the small ranchers was lower down than a snake's ass in a wagon track, but was quite legal. On one of my brand inspection trips to the stock-yards on the P.G.E. I heard a beef buyer blowing real hard, and telling how his company had given him a thousand dollar Christmas present for doing such a real good job of chiselling on prices to the ranchers, so I figured it sure must have paid real good for them. The buyers had all the cattlemen over a barrel anyway.

Late that fall of 1930 at Pine Crest, Peg and I, with Ronnie in bed fast asleep, were sitting talking one evening on the chances of how, where and when we could increase our income. We both realized that these low prices of beef and other farm products were not going to allow us to survive very long, to continue to pay wages, grub bills and taxes and to keep up insurance policies. Each year the ranchers were going deeper and deeper into the hole. If times should pick up again it would take quite a few fair, reasonable years to put us back on our feet again. It sure was a rat race outlook.

Peg said to me, "You know, Harry, I've had an idea for a long time now, that we could go down to the lake and start a fishing and holiday camp for the summer months of each year." I was sure surprised at this but we both sat there and talked over the pros and cons and the problems which would be connected with Peg's idea. After several more talks on the question we decided that we would give it a real try-out, and so we embarked on another side-line to our ranching efforts.

It was towards the end of January 1931, when Peg and I moved down again to Big Bar Lake to begin the guest ranch and fishing camp venture. We had little or no trouble in moving this time, as the lake homestead house was all ready to move into. I got a local boy to stay at Pine Crest and feed the cattle there. I and Peg and little Ronnie all went down to the lake, as we knew we'd have a lot of work to do if we were going to make any headway that coming spring.

I hired a young fellow to help me for the balance of the winter, named Charlie Atkey, who was a real greenhorn, but a willing worker. He had no judgment or experience of any sort or size but as long he had only hard slugging work ahead of him, at which he couldn't make any mistakes, he did all right, and managed to earn the twenty dollars a month and his board that I scraped up for him. It was a prince's salary that winter in the wilderness of the south Cariboo. While not totally cut off from anyone — fifteen miles from your nearest neighbour is quite a little ways out — especially if an emergency deal shows up.

I knew I'd have to cut quite a lot of logs to make a start on the new log cabins we were planning on, so Charlie and I, for around three weeks, used to walk across the lake every morning, with a lunch apiece and our axes. I'd pick out jack-pine trees that were as straight as I could find, cutting them into sixteen- and eighteen-foot lengths. It takes quite a bit of looking and walking around to get real straight jack-pines for a log cabin, because lots of trees look pretty good from a distance, but when you get to them, and look along the tree, you'll find the great majority have some sort of a little bow in them. So I picked out all the trees and cut them down, and Charlie's job was to cut and trim the limbs and branches off. I tried Charlie out at falling the trees down, but he'd almost always wind up falling the tree, hanging it up in the branches and lodging against another tree, which lost lots of time. I'd carefully show him how to size up a tree, as to which way it was leaning, and where to cut his under-cut notch, but he just could not learn somehow. He told me, "Harry, I can't tell which way a tree is going to fall, because I am not a fortune-teller." I just plumb give up trying to tell him, and let him do the tree limbing.

I finally got all the logs cut, and started to skid them up, and to haul two or three sleigh loads across the lake on the ice every day. It was sure a steep bank to go down to the lake from the south side. The team with me on top of the load driving, really used to hit that ice on the lake just a hell-a-hooping but I was lucky and didn't have any upsets or skinning up of any kind coming down that steep bank. Of course I helped it out quite a bit by bringing some fresh horse manure every day or so and sprinkling it in the sleigh tracks coming down the ridge. This slowed things down a little.

Along in the middle of March Charlie and I peeled the bark from these green logs. With Charlie helping me lift logs, I started to lay them up, round-by-round, cutting my notches in the ends of each log kind of careful so I wouldn't have big cracks in the cabin wall. Then when the cabin was ten rounds high, I laid up the ridge logs and got ready to put on a roof of cut poles and a little hay on top of them, and I hauled dirt with the team and wagon later, and threw about eight inches of dirt on them. A door and a window, a board floor, a cook-stove, bed, spring and mattress, some shelves and cupboards Peg made out of some odd boards, and we were just about ready for a customer to start us off in business.

I put up two cabins in the spring of 1931, also an addition to the homestead house which we used for a dining room. It looked real good as Peg got iron oil and I rubbed it on the peeled logs with a cloth, and it made them just shine like polished glass. By and large, we were real proud of our efforts.

The spring and summer of 1931 advanced and we were rewarded by having some fishing-minded folks come to the lake who stayed in our two cabins. I got a friend of mine in Clinton to make us six boats and I managed to buy another three cayuses, so with our three we were able to take in a few holiday guests to ride, fish, swim and just laze around the lake.

In those years we had a couple of good milk cows, and a dozen or more hens, and Peg always raised twenty to thirty turkeys and baked a lot of home-made bread, pies and cakes which sure went over real well with the guests. Our first holiday guests were six school-ma'ams who were very nice girls, and enjoyed their holidays in the wide open spaces and riding on the trails around the lake.

Peg built up the Big Bar Guest Ranch and Fishing Camp all through the years by hard work, long hours and constant attention to the well-being of her guests. She is a past mistress in the art of making people feel completely comfortable — the at-home sort of feeling. I have told her many times that she would have made a fortune for herself if she had gone into the hotel business. Today she owns and operates the Lake Resort entirely on her own, independent of any efforts I make raising cattle and trying to build up a ranch. However, in those first years I did my best to help out all I could, and being raised in a real good home in England till I was sixteen, I always knew a little about good manners and how to say please and thank you, and to act as if I were half-civilized anyway.

In 1932 I figured I'd try and hang on to Charlie for the summer work, as it was getting so that I couldn't handle all the work lone-handed, but Charlie never did improve much in the line of having any gumption about anything which required a little judgment or using his head.

In February I cut out some more jack-pine logs and peeled them, and after the snow had gone and things dried up a bit, I put up another small cabin. I used it for a bunkhouse for many years, and with the exception of the bottom round getting pretty well rotten, the cabin lasted over twenty-eight years, and most of the logs were just as sound as the day they were put in the cabin.

That same year I was able to put the irrigation ditch out of the creek at the head of the lake, down onto the flat of the homestead, which I sowed into a crop of rye hay. I had Charlie irrigate it out of the new ditch I had made, and I cut a good crop of rye hay off the lake field in the latter part of July and early August. When I had finished haying that year I had over one hundred and twenty-five tons at the meadow, the lake and the Pine Crest ranch, and had around ninety head of cattle, counting everything. While it was not at all big, it represented a lot of hard work, and long days.

In the fall of 1932 I was very surprised to receive a letter from my old Commanding Officer of No. 2 Company of the old 158th D.C.O.Rs, Major John Roaf, who was a prominent businessman in Vancouver, asking me if he and a friend could come hunting game-birds around Big Bar Lake with any prospect of success. I was tickled pink to hear from Major Roaf, as all of us who served under him in the days of World War I had a deep and lasting affection for this dignified and square-shooting officer and gentleman. A week or so later a car came to the lake and out stepped "the Honourable Jack Roaf," as I always referred to him.

Major Roaf had a friend with him, a rather short, sturdy and well-built man named Mr. George S. Harrison, who was a Vancouver gentleman of financial standing, and who became an associate of mine over a period of seventeen years, and indeed right up to his death.

It was a little after Major Roaf and Mr. Harrison went back to Vancouver that I got a letter from one of their friends, Mr. Morton W. Morton of Vancouver, who at that time was manager of the Bank of Commerce on Granville Street in Vancouver. Mr. Morton wanted to come to the lake for a month or so's rest and holiday, as he said he had been under a considerable strain, and felt his nerves needed a good quiet change. So he arrived at the lake, and I took him fishing and grouse hunting.

Mort, as we called him, turned out to be a real fellow and we all became great friends over the years that rolled by. He and his missus came to the lake every year for their rest up. I found out that a great many of our leading men were real darned good fellows, and not a pack of human vultures that they are sometimes painted out to be.

I know that as long as Mort was alive, every time I ever happened to be in Vancouver, I'd step up to his big bank on Granville and Hastings Streets and ask the clerk at the desk if I could please see Mr. Morton for a few minutes. Well sir, the way one of those city slicker clerks would kind of throw his nose up in the air when he seen me — sort of had a look on his face that said, "Who in hell drug this fellow in here?" Anyhow, it wouldn't be only a minute or so, and the big glass door would be wide open, and here come Mort out first, with his hand out and a big "Howdy" for me. Believe it or not, the look on the clerk's face just reminded me of a guy with a back-door haemorrhage.

We plugged along that winter. The snow was quite deep but I had lots of hay for our stock, and along in the latter part of February, Peg figured she would have to put ice up for the summer guests, and for fishermen to keep their fish on — so I shovelled the snow off a sizeable piece on the lake, marked it off into squares, and proceeded to cut ice-blocks — about twenty inches square — with an ice-saw, which worked pretty good after we got the first hole started. We made a little wooden slide, and would slide the blocks up this chute onto the sleigh-box and haul the load off the lake and up to a little shed where I stored the ice for summer use, all covered with sawdust. As long as ice is covered with sawdust and no air can get at it, it keeps pretty good.

The spring and summer of 1933 rolled along, and there was little or no change in the depression picture in regard to the cattlemen and the rest of the agricultural producers, all of whom were at the mercy of the packer buyers and the middlemen who were, and still are, the curse of all farming and ranching producers. The middleman toils not, neither does he spin — but makes a nice comfortable profit, doing little or nothing, out of the blood, sweat and tears of a rancher. The only solution to get rid of him would be by nationwide farm co-operatives, however, I will come to this later in the story.

I did run onto one instance in the summer of 1933, where the depression had not affected a fellow's game too much, and it struck me kind of forcibly at the time. One evening at Big Bar Lake a fisherman drove up, a tall, well-built sort of fellow, I'd judge him to be in his early forties, and a kind of serious-faced type of fellow. He stayed several days fishing in which time I had several talks with him in regard to the Big Depression that we were all wallowing in. He very serenely told me that the depression had made little or no difference in his line of business. I was sure puzzled some, and I asked him, "For God's sake, what kind of business are you in?" He told me he was the undertaker in a funeral business in Bellingham, Washington, U.S.A., and so far there had been no big change in his business, to which I agreed that by and large, I guessed that it would be quite normal.

Chapter 12

George Harrison and I Start the OK

IN THE EARLY FALL OF 1933 I had heard that a ranch, down the creek from Big Bar Lake about fourteen miles, was for sale at a very reasonable price. It was an old-time spot, having been once owned by old Joe Haller, who was one of the earliest white men to come to the Big Bar country. I had known of this layout for many years, as it was only seven miles away from the old Crow's Bar pasture where I had put in my first few years for the Gang Ranch. It had some hay and lot of good bunch-grass pasture, and the mail stage to the Gang Ranch run right by the door every week. At this time there was a telephone line running from Clinton to the Gang Ranch along the road — which surely was a real godsend in the matter of getting in touch with the outside world.

My heart was always tied up with a longing to have a good-sized ranch, a pretty good herd of cattle, a pile of good haystacks and grass for the cows. It seemed to me to be a sort of empire-building complex that I had in those days. I have heard it described as the cattleman's itch which amounted to the same thing — always wanting to get bigger and better.

I guess the whole thing in a nutshell is Old Man Ambition everlastingly driving at a fellow to get ahead and get more — just like a squirrel piling up pine cones. Well, it would sure be a poor-looking world if we all set back and didn't take a chance on getting ahead somehow. If I ever hear of a fellow who has no ambition or get-up in his make-up, I just figure he will never set the world on fire at anything and is on the same level as a useless drone in a beehive.

I did quite a bit of meditating as to how and where I could get hold of this property. I finally put on my blue suit, shined up my shoes and combed my hair and went down to Vancouver to find Mr. George S. Harrison who, I was told, was a man of quite a bit of money and might finance me.

After three days of discussion, in which I laid all my cards on the table for him to look at, Mr. Harrison came back to the lake with me. We went down and looked the old Haller place over, and after some more lengthy pow-wows, we agreed to form a small company. We piled up all the different little places — land, cattle, buildings, etc. — into what we called The O K Ranching Co. Ltd., the name being taken from my brand O K on the left ribs which had been my brand for many years.

This opened up a new era in ranching for me. Mr. Harrison and I became lifelong friends over many years until he died and passed over the High Mountain a few years ago. I respected and admired him, just the same as I would have done to my father. He was always the business and financial brains of the O K Ranching Co. Ltd., and on many, many occasions, he played Santa Claus to our hard-working and struggling little company.

It was a good combination, with Mr. Harrison possessing, to his fingertips, the principles and outlines of good business, and a seldom-failing knowledge of human nature. Always an optimist, and always interested in all things going on around him.

I figured I was the practical man — the dependable, long hour, hard-working type that I had been, of necessity, trained to follow. I was never afraid to face an issue, or scared to make a decision. I drove myself hard, and tried to get reasonable value and loyalty from anyone who was working for us. Anytime I had a little brainwave come over me, that I thought would be good for the company, I always submitted it to Mr. Harrison for his judgment.

Our little company had its first start-off on October 8, 1933. Peg and I and Ronnie, who was eight years old, all moved down from the lake to the old Haller place, which became the headquarters layout of the O K Ranching Co.

My first chore was to look around and see if I could buy up "she stuff" to raise up the cattle herd on our O K setup, so I stepped on my Sunny Jim and rode down to the ferry on the Fraser at Big Bar. I rode for about four miles south, on a real jackrabbit trail, till I got to the Chisholm brothers' ranch which is on the west side of the Fraser River.

These two brothers, Willie and Kenny, were a great pair of boys. I had known them for years. You could not find a better or more decent family if you were to ride to Hell and back. They were great horsemen and number one men at packing a horse with a pack that would not loosen up or turn sideways. These boys just naturally had to be good at the pack horse game because their ranch had no road into it, and any supplies they got had to come over the trail, on a pack horse or not at all. Their saddle horses had to be pretty sure-footed, because those narrow sidehill and steep gulch trails along that river was no place for a bumblefoot.

I stayed three days with the boys, and I proposed to buy sixty-odd head of their breeding stock, cows and heifers. After considerable quiet consideration on their part, they agreed to sell them to me. We cut out the bunch and started for the Big Bar ferry, driving them down the trail. They were kind of oily to handle. You could always get a real wild and woolly run out of them if they took a notion. We got them down to the ferry and crossed them over the river and I paid Bill Chisholm. The next day I drove them on up the Big Bar Creek to the O K and a couple of days later saw them all branded with the O K on the left ribs — the brand standing out on them like an old-fashioned privy in a fog.

These Chisholm cows were all more or less mountain-raised stock, none of them real fat, but they had a real good frame on them and when bred to good white-faced bulls they left us some good calves.

I also made a trip to Williams Lake stockyards that fall, and brought back around twenty to thirty good yearling steers which I shipped down from there to the Chasm on the P.G.E. and drove them home to the O K in two long days.

I had two real good men with me at the O K Ranch that winter, with times still pretty tough, at twenty-five dollars a month and their board. One was a pretty tough old customer named Bill Bunnage, who even today is a real mainstay of the O K Ranch. The other fellow was a good local boy named Ernie Love, who was a good hard worker. Bill Bunnage, with whom I had joined our army years before in the World War I, was a man of many parts. In his time Bill had been a sailor, a soldier, a wild horseman, a freighter on the Cariboo Road, a ferryman on the Big Bar ferry, a mail stage driver, a cowboy, and a ranch-hand.

When it came to rough and tumble scraps, there were very few men around the Big Bar and Clinton country who would undertake to give Bill a physical trimming as Bill was a rough tornado in action and knew all the stunts that go with no-rules fighting. Being plumb full of Irish grit, he always figured a way out of any situation that came along. Uncle Bill, as we called him — some of the boys had him nicknamed "Colonel Bill" — had a great pride in always doing his best, and a great loyalty to the O K Ranch, which is one quality in a human being that you can't buy.

Bill really loved to tell about the many hair-raising exploits he'd been into. Sometimes I wondered if he wasn't over exaggerating, and perhaps a little careless with the handling of the truth, but I know that he was sure a tough old customer, and no one could match his stories. In all the years I have known Uncle Bill, I have only heard him out-niggered once. It was at breakfast table one morning at the O K in the late thirties. I had a few men working on the ranch, one of them named Frank Dinger who had been raised in the Utah country in the States, before drifting north to our British Columbia. Frank was a good all-round handyman on a ranch and could turn out pretty near anything in the ranch blacksmith shop.

My friend, Bill, was holding forth and telling us all how good a freight team skinner he was on the Cariboo Road in earlier days, how he had driven teams strung out two-by-two ahead of each other. In fact, they were strung out so far ahead that Uncle Bill had to have a loud megaphone on the wagon seat beside him so that his lead team would hear him calling to them. This Frank Dinger boy, who was a silent sort of fellow, very casually remarked that when he was just a boy on the plains of Kansas, he drove so many teams of oxen strung out two-by-two they damn near stretched as far as the human eye could see. The last team on the wagon tongue, in which he was sitting, driving, were slithering and staggering and weaving up and down and were up to their eyelids in bullshit. Uncle Bill looked at Frank Dinger and just gave a slight cough at that one. Dinger never moved a muscle in his poker face, and I allowed that, it would seem like, to me, that he must have been driving a fair to middlin' long team of oxen.

In the winter of 1933 we had to take a lot of our cattle up to Pine Crest to feed, which was now twenty-eight miles from the O K headquarters, so Uncle Bill loaded up his sleigh with grub and blankets and drove the team ahead of the cattle, who strung along out behind in the sleigh tracks. After the haystacks were fed out at Pine Crest, we brought the cattle down to Big Bar Lake and continued to feed them there.

Towards the first week of March the snow got pretty soft and melting on the mountain about a couple of miles above the O K headquarters, and a lot of waving grass showed up in the last four inches of snow, so I turned out about thirty head of coming-two-year-old steers up in a real good pasture field, figuring they could get all the grass they needed without any hay feeding. They were all in fair shape and I hoped to ship them in early August before the prices started to drop, which meant that I'd probably get at least fifteen dollars a head more for them as against keeping them till October when the big run of beef cattle comes on to the market.

One afternoon I sent Ernie Love up on the mountain to take a ride around those steers and see if they were all right, and had a couple of blocks of salt to lick. Ernie came back, in an hour or so, riding on the run to tell me he was sure some of those steers were sick. A few minutes later he and I were riding to beat hell up to look at those steers. I saw some of these steers in very evident distress — their hair stood out, their eyes were glaring and bugged out, and every little while one would fall down, and stagger up again with all four feet braced outwards. A lot of them would pass out a long thin string of very strong smelling manure. Ernie and I gathered up the steers and brought them all down to the ranch and I cut out twenty of them who certainly were very sick and kept them in the yard back of the barn.

These steers acted to me like they had eaten something poisonous but I sure couldn't figure out what it could be. I got a few bottles of glycerine and drenched them hoping that it would smooth out their stomachs, ease their pain, but one by one, out of the twenty affected, sixteen died.

This was a rough jolt. I was sure worrying to beat hell as I knew we needed the cheque for the steers in August, and being dead there would be no pay from them. I wired Mr. Harrison in Vancouver, telling him the story and asking him to please contact the Dominion Veterinary Department in Vancouver, and to please send a vet up at once, as we were in real trouble. The department sent up an elderly vet called Dr. Jernyrs, who reached the O K away late at night. The next morning, right after breakfast, he cut one of the dead steers open and informed me that the steers died of haemorrhagic septicaemia which was more or less known as cattle stomach flu. He told me to get some vaccine at once, and inoculate all the cattle on the ranch.

I disagreed entirely with this diagnosis. I had had previous experience at the Canoe Creek Ranch and the Gang Ranch with this cattle stomach flu before, but I felt that I could not put myself up as knowing more than a government veterinary doctor and so I sent a wire to Calgary for enough vaccine to inoculate around one hundred and ninety head. I got a message through to the postmaster at Clinton asking him, by every means, to see that the vaccine was sent out by the mail stage which was due three days later, as we sure needed it. It did not arrive, and two or three days later after a lot of desperate phone calls to Clinton, I got word that the vaccine had arrived at Clinton post office. I made up my mind that I was going to get that vaccine and inoculate all the cattle on the ranch, following the vet's instructions.

I telephoned a great friend of mine, Mr. James Robertson, who, with his brother Raymond was the owner of the famous Robertson Brothers' store in Clinton. I arranged for him to pick up the vaccine from the post office, and I'd be at his house to get it sometime that night.

I got Peg to get me a couple of cups of coffee and some sandwiches. Then I went out and saddled up a little bay mare. I called her Babe. She sure was a dandy little mare to ride as she had a fast running walk, which was just what I wanted to go over the miles. I told Peg I'd be back by morning, and not to worry. At half-past three in the afternoon I stepped up on Babe and started for Clinton, thirty-eight long miles through the snow, and a lot of high mountain country to ride over. You climb to nearly five thousand feet on the road from the O K on Big Bar Creek and dip down again at Kelly Lake, but lucky for me the road was broke all the way.

I knew that I had to watch the strength and the ginger in this little mare because I had the return ride to make, and I'd told Peg I'd be back come early morning. If you ever tell anyone in our country you'll be there on a certain day and don't come, you have everyone wondering what's happened, if you are hurt or something, and they'll maybe start looking for you. If you just say you'll be back as soon as you can, then people don't expect you to come along until you're good and ready and nobody worries.

I kept up a steady even gait all the way, the snow was fairly well packed down in the sleigh tracks, and along about ten o'clock that night I arrived in Clinton. My little mare was tired some, but not too tired. I put her in the big livery barn on the upper end of the town, and fed her some hay and grain. After having downed some hot coffee and ham and eggs in the restaurant, which was just about closing up for the day, I walked up to Jim Robertson's house and got my vaccine.

I rested my little mare for an hour and a half, then put the vaccine package right underneath my undershirt next to my hide, figuring that would keep the vaccine from freezing. I said "So long" to my friend, Jim, and his missus, walked up to the barn, stepped up on my little mare and started to ride home on the thirty-eight mile trip.

I decided that I would ride by the lake road instead of taking the Kelly Lake road over the mountain. I knew the road was broken, and I knew that Uncle Bill was at Big Bar Lake feeding some of our cattle there. So I rode on, mile after mile through the darkness with only a few stars shining, hoping all the time that my saddle mare would not play out. As the morning hours came along I could feel the cold settling down in the night air and my mare's feet rang out more clearly as they plugged along the frozen sleigh track. Along about three that morning I rode into the Big Bar Lake, put my mare in the barn, and went into the house to wake Uncle Bill up. I told him the story of the dead steers and he shook his head and said, "That'll sure raise old blue Morman Jesus with you, Harry." I said, "Yes, it sure will, Uncle. There's no money in dead cattle."

Bill had a brown horse called Blaze in the barn at the lake, so I traded horses with him, leaving little Babe at the lake. I pushed along the last fourteen miles of the trip, riding into the O K at around half-past five in the morning, having made the round trip of seventy-six miles in fourteen hours. Boy-oh-boy, they were long, long hours in the snow, cold and darkness.

I walked up to the house, and Peg already had the cook-stove going and hot coffee waiting for me. As soon as I had eaten, Ernie and I and two other local boys corralled the cattle and I inoculated them for septicaemia with a hypodermic needle. I was so dog tired and weary that night that I fell asleep at the supper table. However, still being reasonably young, in my early forties, I was none the worse for the trip after a good night's rest. It was a tough, wearing experience, as it was normally a two-day ride. Yet it had to be done. Anyone living in these isolated parts of our wide open Cariboo had to school himself to meet any kind of an emergency. It was well to follow the philosophy and the grit of the old mountain men who, when rough stuff hit them, which was often and regular at times, pinned their ears back, set their faces, buttoned their lips and took what came without complaint or hollering blue ruin. I always felt kind of glad in my own mind, that I belonged to that hardy and resourceful bunch — the kind that never hollers whoa until the wagon is upside down.

I was feeling kind of worried and discouraged over the loss of those fine young steers as I had had hopes of getting around forty dollars a head for them as beef in August. I said to young Ernie one day out in the barn, "Ernie, I don't know what I'm going to do for money to pay you and Bill now I've lost those steers." The damn good lad just looked at me for a few seconds and then said, "Well, Harry, don't worry about me, I'll wait for mine." That brightened up the picture quite a bit, and I got to thinking the sun would get to shining on both sides of the fence after awhile maybe.

Chapter 13

OK Beef for Bralorne Mines

I STILL FIGURED in my mind that those steers had not died from any kind of septicaemia or cattle flu, so I said to Peg one morning, "Honey, I'm going to take a butcher knife out there, and I'm going to get some guts out of one of those steers and send them to the Government Laboratory down at Victoria and get them analyzed and see what they say." So I cut one of them open and took a sample of his stomach and the stomach lining, put it in a large tin can and shipped it down on the P.G.E. train going through Kelly Lake.

I then drug all the dead steers up on a rock pile in a little meadow above the ranch building. I hauled all the old stumps, rotten fence posts and brush I could gather up, piled them on top of the steers and set fire to the bunch. Of course there was quite a strong stench rose up from the pile, but by burning them I figured I would stop any chance of infection arising.

It was about ten days after I had sent down the tin can with the insides in it that I got a wire from Victoria telling me that the analysis of the insides convinced them that the steers had died of poisoning, probably arsenical poisoning. So I was convinced that the veterinary surgeon was entirely wrong in his judgment. All the long seventy-six mile ride to Clinton and back in the night for the vaccine was wasted after all. However, it was just one of those things that can come along, and I was at a loss to ever get the absolute truth, rock-bottom proof, of the arsenic in that pasture. I knew that grasshopper poison, which contains arsenic, had been well scattered around that pasture a few years earlier, but I could never find any of it. Since that time, in the last three years, a very poisonous weed called arrow grass has been found right close to the lake, and this might have been the cause.

The spring of 1934 was well advanced and found me busy putting in some crops in addition to the tame hay and wild meadow hay we had. We planted about one hundred acres on Big Bar Mountain into wheat and oats, trusting that the good Lord would send us some rain in the right time, so we'd get some dry farm crop. There were still half a dozen homesteaders left on Big Bar Mountain at that time and they were getting by, but that's about all. The summer found us buying out an old-timer named Grant Lee, who had originally come from Texas, and had a place about two miles up the road from the O K headquarters. This little addition gave us another sixty-odd tons of good clover and timothy hay. Grant was a very careful type of fellow and counted every nickel several times over before he ever spent it. He always refused to lend anybody any money because there were quite a few bums and borrowers around that settlement who never figured to pay any debt, if they could scheme a way out of it. Grant was about the only man in the settlement of Big Bar who had any cash money at all.

The day by day routine of ranch work, and the regular attention to the many things involved in trying to build up a ranch and make it win, or at least break even, took up all my time and effort, so I gave up my job as Brand Inspector and the old 59 Mile House, and the stockyards at the Chasm and Lone Butte, which were very familiar landmarks to me for over a matter of seven years.

For years at the 59 Mile House, there was an elderly bachelor named George Fairbairn, who owned the layout which in early days was quite a stopping place for freighters and their teams, and at one time the house had a liquor bar. George had been a prospector for most of his years, was very set in his ways, and he seemed to take a great dislike to anyone with a car, or with a good suit of clothes on him. George wouldn't serve any meals except to cowboys and cattlemen who were never very fussy about what they ate, just as long as there was lots of it, and they never had any choosey ways of eating or sleeping.

Now George was bothered considerable with eye troubles, he had one glass eye, but managed to get along with his good eye. On one occasion when he agreed to cook dinner for a bunch of cowboys and cattlemen who were shipping cattle at the stockyards, George figured he'd do the cowboys real proud by cooking them a pot of dried prunes. The boys wolfed down a big feed of boiled beef, spuds, beans and hot biscuits, and each man took his saucer and loaded it up with the cooked prunes as a sort of dessert when one of the boys named Leonard McCarty, who was driving the beef-buyer around in a car, ground his teeth real hard on what he figured was a prune stone, but when he spit it out he found he had been chewing on George's glass eye. But anyway, George wiped off the glass eye and slipped it back in the empty eye socket, and everybody got a real good-natured laugh out of that.

In the spring of 1934 Peg had gone back to Big Bar Lake to continue on with the guest ranch and fishing camp business, as no one else could ever look after that game anything like as good as she could. I, of course, had to stay at the ranch headquarters and look after things there, as both the lake and the O K needed a lot of attention and careful managing, otherwise you maybe could run into careless and unnecessary bills and expenses.

I've always found that if a guy owns anything or any business of any kind, it pays big to have the personal look-see over it. In my experience in the cow business I've always found that absentee ownership is sure a damn poor game because no one looks after what you own better than yourself. Relying on others to look after your business is a very poor system to get into. The eye of the master is the best bet you can have for success.

I used to ride up to the Lake every week or two, to see how Peg was getting along, and every so often she'd be down to the O K. Sometimes she'd ride down with her guests and sometimes she'd come alone and do a big washing for me and Ronnie.

I sent Ernie Love up to the lake that summer. He was sure a fine boy to help out in the many chores and things that had to be done, although he told me that he didn't like it up there. I got him to stay the season anyway.

We had lots of rain that year and the dry farm crops really did grow, and the grain ripened good, and the hay crop was a lot better than average, so things began to take on a little better look for us all, and I for one was truly thankful for that.

In September of 1934 when my partner, Mr. Harrison, was up at the ranch on one of his visits — which were several times in a summer and maybe once in the winter — I approached him one evening in the sitting room at the house with a brainwave which had been churning around in my old head for quite a long time.

I suggested to Mr. Harrison, who knew all the high moguls and the directors of the Bralorne Mines in the Bridge River area not far from Lillooet, that perhaps our O K company, through Mr. Harrison's efforts, could butcher their own beef and ship them dressed to the Bralorne mines each week. That way we'd get the financial gravy for ourselves instead of that greedy meat-packer getting it down in Vancouver. I told Mr. Harrison that I figured I was a pretty fair butcher, and had had a lot of experience in butchering beef and hogs, and dressing out turkeys. At that time the O K had a very respectable slaughter house on the ranch, with a cement floor included.

Mr. Harrison looked at me long and hard for a minute or so after me having put up my idea, and said he would meditate considerable on the idea. In those years Mr. Harrison was a personal friend of the famous Major Austin Taylor of Vancouver, who was the absolute top bracket of the Bralorne Mines Company. I had the pleasure of meeting him on one occasion at the O K when he called on Mr. Harrison, and Major Taylor impressed me as being a strong silent man of very far-seeing penetration and observation.

A few days after I had advanced the notion of butchering our own beef, Mr. Harrison jumped in his car and drove over to Bralorne Mines, which was quite a drive, and returned late at night. I was sitting up in the kitchen at the O K with the coffee pot on the stove and a hot meal handy for him, waiting for the verdict as to whether they would take our beef or not. When Mr. Harrison had downed a couple of cups of scalding hot coffee, he told me that the manager at the Bralorne Mines had agreed to take one dressed steer as a trial shipment from the O K Ranching Co. Ltd., at a date named for October 8, 1934 — which date was somewheres about two weeks' time away.

I decided that I would take a flying trip to Vancouver, so Peg and I drove her little car down there, and I became a visitor at a meat packing plant for a few hours, with the idea in my head to perhaps pick up any new ideas, or details of butchering and dressing out carcasses of beef, that I was not wise to. I saw the manager of a large meat packing concern in Vancouver — one that we had shipped cattle to by live weight — and I asked him if I could look around the plant in which quite a few of our cattle through the years had walked their last few feet alive.

The manager most generously told a man to show me around, and let the country boy see how they handled the beef butchering. My old head was aturning sideways just like it was working automatic, taking in everything I could see and hear, and Peg and I returned to the ranch with a lot of new ideas and information which sure were very valuable to me in the new move in the beef business.

There never was a departed king, emperor, high priest, or any other kind of a mogul that ever had more close care and attention than what I gave to that trial shipment of that steer's carcass for the Bralorne Mines. It was sure a fat well-dressed-out carcass of beef — all turned out in the latest style. Mr. Harrison accompanied that trial-dressed steer all the way to the Bralorne Mines.

We had to take the beef twenty-seven miles, from the O K to Kelly Lake station on the P.G.E. It was put in the express car and unloaded at Shalalth, which was about twelve miles below Lillooet station. The meat was then taken by a trucking line, run by an old friend of mine named Curly Evans. The road to Bralorne Mines, going up over Mission Mountain, was sure a steep heavy graded climb. I was sure plumb surprised at the heavy loads of freight that passed over that steep mountain, and I'd say that any truck driver that could drive up and down that mountain sure knew his business.

There was some doubt on the part of the Bralorne Mine officials that the O K Company would be able to deliver the beef on the same well-finished scale that they had got from the Meat Packing Co. Mr. Harrison told me of this and finished up by saying, "Son, I told them over at Bralorne that you were the best butcher this side of Mexico — now don't let me down, because any miscues you make will just stick up like a sore thumb."

Well, Sir, God bless old George Harrison! He had more drive and go-gettedness than any man I have ever known, and I've known a whole pile of real good men in my time.

With this whirlwind of a reputation as a butcher, my mind was made up to be not only good, but top-hand good. Through a period of eight years of supplying that fine mine their beef and a lot of their pork, I will say that we gave a fine record of service to them, and they proved to be real grand people to do business with.

The final result arrived by telegram from Bralorne. It gave us a weekly order of two carcasses of dressed beef every week, and sometimes three, which was a pretty good order for a little company like ours.

In the late fall of 1934 I got hold of the best all-around man I have ever run across. He was a young, square shouldered boy, named Jack Tresierra, born and raised in our Big Bar Creek area. His father was from an old family of pioneers in the early days of Big Bar and the Williams Lake area. Jack was a very quiet and modest young man, a top-hand at all and any outside work, especially at building or constructing anything, and it seemed like that nothing could stick him. I honestly believe that starting from scratch, Jack could hew out a set of leggings for a humming-bird if he had to. The O K company surely owed Jack a heavy debt of gratitude for the many things he did while he was with us.

We had a more or less easy winter and around March, 1935, the snow disappeared and the bare ground showed up again, and I got busy for what I knew would be a real busy spring and summer. We had a hydro-electric light plant at the O K which gave us lights, ran a water pump and a few odds and ends, and in the early spring we installed a methyl-hydrate cooling system in our slaughter house which worked very well. By this means we kept our beef carcasses at a little below 32° in the meat cooler all spring, summer and fall. In the winter months the good Lord with his winter weather took care of the meat temperatures, as the O K Ranch was one of the outstanding places in the Cariboo for sub-zero temperatures, the reason being that the buildings were laying between two bunch-grass hills, and close to Big Bar Creek which seemed to draw the cold air all the time to the low-laying creek bottom. As old Uncle Bill used to say, "Summer times it is hotter than the hinges of hell, and winter time it is colder than a step-mother's breath."

In April of 1935 a solid built young man, named Edwin Loring, came to work at the O K. He was the grandson of an old pioneer family, the Lorings of Lytton, down on the junction of the Fraser and Thompson Rivers. Edwin turned out to be a Grade A all-around man. Through thick and thin, good days and bad, Edwin has remained very closely with the family. He still is the great mainstay of the Lake Guest Ranch which Peg was running for the company at that time, but which she purchased from the O K in later years.

I also added two more boys from the local area, Joe Bishop and Joe Murdock, both of them real good men. Joe Bishop was really a wizard at truck driving and keeping it in shape. Every week we had to take out the beef for Bralorne — each Tuesday night — but in the winter months we used a team and sleigh to get the beef to Kelly Lake, as in those years there were no snow ploughs to clear the road of snow whenever it came down good and heavy, which it often did.

The spring break-up on the road to Kelly Lake really caused me a lot of worry in the matter of the weekly shipment of beef. It had to go through regardless, and that's where Joe Bishop really did shine. He could get there and stay out of bog-holes better than anyone I ever seen. Breakdowns are real expensive and if the meat truck ever had to be pulled out with a wrecker and hoist from Clinton, you could get yourself ready to write out a real big cheque.

As soon as the snow had gone off the fields on Big Bar Mountain we started to put in our dry farm crop of wheat and oats. I had Uncle Bill, who was in command at the camp on the mountain, and Joe Murdock and another fellow, called Henry Hinck, who was a good fellow except that he moved so slow. He put me in mind of a fellow who has got to the toilet at least two to five minutes too late. Nothing but an earthquake could have changed that slow gait, and maybe that wouldn't have been enough either.

I used to drive the little truck from the O K buildings after supper every night, to their camp with grub and odds and ends. One night I got up there and said to Bill, "Well, Uncle, how's she been going today?" To which Uncle replied, "Not worth a damn, Harry. I've been as sick as a dog today. Are you sure that beef liver you brought up yesterday was good?" I told Bill I was sure the liver was all right. Uncle Bill shook his head and said he had sure been avomiting. The next night when I was up Bill told me he had found the cause of the trouble. It turned out that Joe Murdock had been using some old harness oil to grease the skillet when frying the morning hotcakes. The trouble was soon remedied by using bacon grease instead.

With our beef business off to a good start, it became necessary to find ways and means to recover as much of the by-products of our beef animals as we could. I have always been told that the only thing the packer couldn't use in butchering pigs, was the squeal, and with the beef animals he couldn't do anything with the steer's beller, but I guess he got all the rest. However, we couldn't quite compare our little outfit to a meat packer in the matter of disposal of all the by-products as we had no method of recovering from the feet and heads of the beef. The beef hides were very carefully salted down, the salt being spread over the flesh side of the hide. This method preserved the gelatine on the flesh side which is a very necessary factor to the leather tanning trade.

Twice a year, spring and fall, we sent hides down to Vancouver where they were sold to a gentleman named Pierre Paris, who owned and operated a tanning and shoe-making business in Vancouver. Mr. Paris always gave us a pretty fair price for the beef hides, and we'd kill two birds with one stone by loading up with supplies on the return trip home.

Our top-hand, Jack Tresierra, really went into action in the summer of 1935 and put up a cow house and two hog houses, all out of logs. Mr. Harrison insisted they were hog palaces which indeed they were. We purchased six brood sows from the famous Colony Farm close to New Westminster. All of them were bred.

They were of the Yorkshire breed and were fine sows, long and deep and short-legged. They were good mothers, and over the years that strain of sows produced us a lot of fine pork.

Mr. Harrison shipped me up a large round boiler — cut in half — which I mounted on a rock fireplace. All the insides of the beef carcasses (with the exception of the liver, heart and tongue) were cooked up in this boiler and mixed with some grain and small spuds, whenever I could get them. This mixture boiled up and cooled, sure did make a real dish for our sows and their litters. However, I think this mix was better for the growing pigs than for sows with very young litters.

The one hog palace was used for the brood-sows to farrow in, and raise their litter till they were around eight weeks old. The second hog palace was used to feed and finish the young growing hogs. I sure took a lot of real care of our brood-sows, especially at the time of their farrowing. It takes three months, three weeks and three days for a sow to have youngsters, and if a lot of care is not taken when they are being born, a number of the little pigs will get layed on, or tromped on, especially in the case of a young sow. Like all classes of animals and human beings too, the births occurred mostly at night between eleven and five o'clock. Nine times out of ten I used to be personally around sitting up with the sow. I figured it paid off big.

I had a stove in the farrowing house, and as fast as the young pig would emerge from the "oven" I'd dry it off with an old sack and gently put it on its ma's teats, which was their lunch counter and means of survival. I always found that gently rubbing a sow's belly, back and forth with your hand, had a very calming down and soothing effect, and I do know that if I had gone to bed, left the sow and let nature take its own course, I'd have often found several young pigs dead in the morning, which sure didn't pay. Today they have brought out special farrowing crates which have cut out all the painstaking efforts I used to do in those days.

We produced a lot of fine, fat and sturdy hogs and, from September to May of each year, we sent dressed pork to our Bralorne Mines customers. Each spring and fall I'd make a personal trip in to Bralorne, and talk things over with the businesslike and genial Mr. Ashmore, who controlled all the food purchases of that large gold-mining operation. In all the years we supplied that fine company with meat we had very agreeable dealings all around. For them, as well as ourselves.

In the meanwhile, Peg was really doing well at the Lake Guest Ranch, and Edwin had cut out a considerable pile of jack-pine logs, and hauled them out. The summer of 1935 saw a very nice addition to the lodge put up, a good fireplace built, and some extra rooms for guests. There was a very attractive sitting room for the many different folks who came there on holiday or for fishing. Sometimes Peg would have as many as twenty-six guests there at one time.

Peg had to have extra help to lift some of the work off her shoulders. She'd generally get one or two of the local girls if possible, and sometimes I'd be able to send someone up to help Edwin on the busy days. I always kept the guest ranch supplied with beef and pork from the O K headquarters.

The dry farm crop on Big Bar Mountain turned out real well that year which was a great help to us, as our meat business called for grain-fed cattle between November and July each year. The steady even shipment of beef each week made it necessary for us to buy extra replacement steers as we did not have enough cattle on the ranch at that time to meet the amount of beef we needed, so I used to have to buy quite a few young steers each year and finish them off on the ranch, to keep our meat business supplied.

In the early part of October 1935, I went down to Ashcroft and took the C.P.R. to Calgary and went around the big stock-yards looking for some good cows. After a day or so I went out to a ranch near Airdrie and purchased ninety-three real top Hereford cows and brought them home to the O K. It took about six days to drive them up from Ashcroft, where I had unloaded them out of the railroad car. Uncle Bill and Mr. Harrison's boy, young George, who was at the O K helping me to run it, came down to Ashcroft leading my saddle horse so we brought them all home without any real trouble. Those cows increased our herd considerable in the matter of a year or so. They were just the kind of cows to produce a good husky calf, which made a marked improvement on the ranch herd.

November 1935 came along and I got an invitation from Mr. Harrison to come down to Vancouver and bring Uncle Bill with me, as he wanted to take Bill and I, with some of his friends, on a hunting trip along the coast. This sounded fine to me, as I had never been on the Pacific Ocean in my life and I knew it would be a great change and a chance to see some new country.

So Bill and I high-tailed it to Vancouver and that evening we got on board Mr. Harrison's gasoline-powered boat, the *Nora Jane*, named after his second daughter who was sure a real fine little lady. He told me that we had nothing to bring in the way of supplies, except that I'd have to have my own chewing tobacco, as he didn't use it. There were three personal friends of Mr. Harrison as well as himself; Mr. Pete Gordon, Mr. Tom Trapp and Mr. Ernie Burns, all Vancouver businessmen. An old sailor named Captain Walter Dass was in charge of the ship.

The first morning out at sea, Bill and I were laying in our bunks listening to the throb of the ship's motors, and the swell of the waves lapping up alongside the boat. I had woke up pretty early by force of habit and Bill was awake too and puffing away at his old pipe — looking pretty contented looking — when the cabin door opened and in come a steward fellow with a large tray in his hand full of bacon and eggs, toast and coffee. I rared up out of my bunk and said to this waiter boy, "Look at here, old-timer, you don't have to pack my breakfast in to me. I'm man enough to get up and eat my grub at a table anytime." The steward told me that it was Mr. Harrison's orders that Bill and I were to have our breakfasts in bed.

Bill looked at me kind of wise looking and said, "Harry, if I'd ever knew I was going to get into an outfit like this, I'll go to hell if I wouldn't have went out and bought me a toothbrush." I allowed to Bill that I guessed that we'd got right into high society. That trip up there was quite a change for me, nothing to do but sail along. We kept on crawling up the coast, and done some hunting — birds mostly. One inlet we stopped at was called Klemtu Passage, and I rowed Mr. Gordon and Bill in a rowboat to the shore to hunt. Well, sir, I never did see so much rain come down in such a short time, and I couldn't help but think how fine it would be if those rains would keep on going over to our interior where they would really do some good, instead of falling down on thick brush and rock slopes right down to the edge of the salt water.

We turned back at a place just south of the Gardner Canal, and on the way back the *Nora Jane* called in at Powell River, and we were shown over the big paper plant there. They were sure turning out a lot of paper of all kinds, heading out to all points of the earth, I guess. I was not very struck with that country going up along the coast, as I never saw a piece of ground level enough that you could spread a saddle-blanket over it, without wrinkling up the edges. If there was any, a man would probably have a job clearing off the big stumps and thick underbrush. However, I guess the timber business and the fishing business does all right in there. I had a real good trip and a change, but was glad to get back to the O K, and glad I was a cowboy and not a waterman.

Chapter 14

Sixty Below . . . the Howling Dog and Gold

I HAD HARDLY GOT BACK from the trip up the coast when trouble and bitching reared up its ugly head in the shape of some sickness breaking out in among our calves. The ailment was coccidiosis, which is a bug that is picked up by the calf. It takes fourteen days to incubate, and by that time the germs are there by the million in the calf's stomach. The calf would pass out strings of blood in his manure, and would sometimes take fits, throw himself down and grind his teeth.

I doctored them up by drenching them with a beer-bottle full of a mixture of sulphate of iron, sulphur and salol, and we finally got it checked but, as time went on, we found that we had been using the wrong dope for it. The great Lederle Chemical Company brought out a dope in tablet form called sulfa guanidine which sure knocked the coccidiosis bug in a matter of three or four days. That sickness has been a sure expensive one. I remember the Gang Ranch losing over four hundred head of calves with it, one winter. When I saw a calf straining, or one with a dirty tail, I was sure on the look out, and watched for signs of blood in their manure.

In January 1936, Jack Tresierra got out a lot of logs on the mountain behind the O K, ready for more buildings in the spring. All the additions and improvements in these years would not have been possible without the financial help and long-headed judgment of my friend and associate, Mr. Harrison, who with his keen and wide-awake business brain, made it possible for us to build up the layout.

Springtime arrived and we had the usual big run and hustle and bustle to get our work well organized and going. That year we sowed around two hundred acres on that Big Bar Mountain, wheat, oats and barley, hoping that the good Lord would drop some rain on the crop up there. Our dressed meat game to the Bralorne Mines was by far the most important nerve in our ranch progress. It was "The Business" as far as we were concerned.

At this time I got another small brainwave which I put up to Mr. Harrison for his final word. The idea was to butcher an extra beef each week and supply meat orders direct to home owners and businessmen in Clinton. There were quite a few folks there who used from three pounds to a quarter of beef every week in homes, restaurants and hotels. Mr. Harrison thought the idea was real good and only made one remark saying, "Harry, it's the one that pays that makes the best customer," which was sure enough the truth.

I made a personal house-to-house call on all and any who I thought would be interested in getting a piece of beef or pork delivered to their homes in Clinton every week. The result was that I added another twenty-five customers or more to my meat list.

Every late Tuesday night our meat would leave the O K headquarters and be taken to catch the south-bound P.G.E. on the early Wednesday morning. After the quarters of beef were put on the P.G.E. express car, our truck would leave for Clinton and deliver our weekly meat orders. I gave my customers good, reliable and clean service. On the return trip the truck always brought back any grub required for the ranch from the famous Robertson Brothers' store.

The two brothers, James and Raymond, were a pair of fine reliable boys and they developed a business which was a mainstay to the whole area. There were many settlers and ranchers, both big and small, who were greatly benefited by the generous credit accounts given them by these square-shooting brothers. In all my years in the South Cariboo I have never known of one instance where a real worthwhile, hard-working settler was refused credit in the line of buying a sack of flour and necessary grub. Robertson Brothers became, and still are, a real institution in the economic life of our South Cariboo area.

Summer came along and our top-hand, Jack Tresierra, put up a new ranch bunkhouse and cook-house combined, which was a much-needed improvement. I turned the old bunkhouse into an office and a storeroom. I got me a desk with a few sliding-door cupboards made and generally at night-times I'd catch up with our ranch accounts and keep track of what Mr. Harrison called "the ins and outs." He always said to be sure there were a little more "ins" than there were "outs," and I sure done my damndest to have it that way.

Jack also put up a big log house for Mr. Harrison about eight hundred yards from the O K buildings on a high ridge above Big Bar Creek. It was the best log house I have ever seen and will be standing there when Judgment Day comes along. It sure is an outstanding mark of Jack Tresierra's top-hand ability. The O K Ranch Company, of course, could not afford to pay the wages that a man of Jack's ability was worth, so in the fall of 1936 Jack left the ranch and took a course in engineering in Vancouver. We all sure hated to see him go. Today, Jack has a shop-foreman's job in a big truck manufacturing company. He has remained a very personal friend all through the years and he will always be remembered by the folks of the Big Bar country.

The dry farm crops that year were a total and dismal failure. It was a real hot dry summer with no rain of any sort over a period of ten weeks during the growing season. The grass on the range burnt right up and withered. The springs were almost dry and clouds of dust were everywhere, stirred up by those hot warm winds. This picture looked so bad that I bought an extra hundred tons of hay at Meadow Lake about twenty-five miles from the OK.

To climax the picture, we had an eight-inch fall of snow in the first ten days of November, and from then on we all knew what a rough, tough winter was like. The snow got real deep and we had at least six weeks of fifty-below-zero weather — and sometimes lower. The only time the thermometer improved was around the middle of the day when the temperature would generously rise to about twenty degrees above zero. As soon as the sun went down — down she'd drop again to forty-odd below.

The road to Kelly Lake was really deep with snow and each week it took a long tough return trip for the team and sleigh. The team would be just covered with white frost on their hair and harness. On one occasion I left the ranch when it was sixty-two below zero. It was the coldest day I have ever seen in my time — colder than a bank manager's hand. The sleigh runners just growled and groaned as they slid along in that Arctic temperature. I tied the reins up on the sleigh box and walked behind in the sleigh tracks almost all the way to Kelly's Lake, which was twenty-seven long miles.

I stopped the team at a little creek called Dry Lake which was a little more than halfways, and figured I'd give them some hay and a feed of grain that I had on the sleigh. There were icicles five inches long just ahanging from their nostrils and tinged with blood. I broke off the icicles but the team just stood there not caring to eat. I didn't eat either, as the sandwich I had in my pocket was frozen solid and there were no dry brush branches near where I could get a fire started. I remember sticking my axe down in the snow straight up, and the end of the handle was out of sight. I smiled to myself, thinking that if Admiral Byrd and some of those other polar observers had ever known about that Dry Lake Mountain, they could have saved themselves a lot of time, travel and aggravation by coming to Dry Lake, because that is surely in a North Pole setting if there ever was one.

Nevertheless, I kept inching along the road hoping, and whispering up to the good Lord, that neither the team nor myself would play out in the last twelve miles. Mile after mile I kept crawling along. I finally got to Kelly Lake about half-past nine that night. My old friend, Bill Birdsell at Kelly Lake Ranch, was waiting for me to show up. I looked after the horses first. Then the coffee and scalding hot vegetable soup soon brought me around again to a reasonable warmth. Bill helped to put the beef on the train — the beef frozen solid as a rock — and I went up to his house and got into a warm bed. After a good sleep and a big breakfast I started back again for the O K Ranch, getting there that evening.

It was sure a tough trip on the horses and me included, but I made it in the same frame of mind I had been trained to do — the old mountain men style. It had to be done and nothing was gained by feeling sorry for yourself. The old saying, "Hell has no terrors for a cowboy," is sure the truth.

We lost fifteen cows that winter. Most of them were poor thin cows late in the fall, and although I did everything I could for them, fed them lots of hay and some grain besides, it seemed like the intense cold just went right through them. Whenever they would lay down in the late afternoon — the sun going down like a ball of red fire far away — with the frosty grey-coloured mountains all pointed for another night of forty-odd below zero, these cows could hardly get up on their feet in the morning. So one by one, the cows give up all hope and died. You can darned near always tell when a cow is going to die, her eyes get kind of glassy and she just quits trying.

Before the end of April 1937 arrived, we were hauling hay from Meadow Lake, which was over twenty-two miles away, to feed our beef cattle. As a rule it is always the best plan to drive the cattle to the haystacks rather than haul the hay to them, but the beef cattle that we were killing for our meat business had by necessity to be kept at home.

I sure had a real hair-raising experience on Big Bar Lake that winter. I brought up around one hundred and eighty head of cattle, as we had some stacks of hay at the lake to be fed out, so we started in the morning from the O K and along about four in the afternoon we were real close to the lake, and I figured that if we drove them across the snow-covered lake it would save us at least two miles. I had often rode my horse across the lake on the ice in the winter so I and the other two boys turned the cattle down onto the lake, which was around seven hundred yards across, and figured we'd make quite a short-cut.

The cattle got well out in the middle of the lake and started to bunch up all together, acting like they didn't want to go, and I saw to my dismay that they were standing in six inches or more of water which was beneath the snow. I got really excited as I realized there must be an airhole or two in the ice, and with the great weight of these cattle the water must have poured up out of the airholes and started to flood over the ice under the snow. I felt it was just nip-and-tuck. If the ice broke through most of the cattle would drown.

Well, sir, with Edwin Loring's help and a fellow called Quin Abel, we managed to string the cattle out by twos and threes across the lake. That way we distributed the weight pretty good, and by good luck and Providence, we crossed them all safely. It was with a thankful prayer to God that I saw the last critter off that ice and heading along for a feed of hay. I have never tried that again, and never will either. Since that time I have always kept to the shoreline of the lake, even when riding a saddle horse. It sure don't pay to take too many chances, as you don't always win.

The long, hard winter of 1936, like everything else in the game of life, finally petered out in April, and I was real glad to see the snow melting and the run-off water tearing down the sidehills and the gulches. You could tell by looking at them how glad our cows were to quit eating dry hay, and to look for the early green grass just about ready to start growing.

In that spring, Mr. Harrison and I received several letters from some Vancouver folks who wanted us to take over a mortgage they held on the old Grinder Ranch on the river at Big Bar. They said that my old friend, Billy Grinder, had signed over all his interests to them some time previously and they were searching around for anyone who would take over the mortgage and ranch, so that sooner or later they might get their money out of it. This called for a lot of meditating and studying of their offer to us. After quite a lot of discussion on the question, we decided we would take a chance and take over the ranch. Billy moved up to a little place several miles up Big Bar Creek, and has been quite comfortable, and has had no worries ever since.

At this time, the old Grinder place was in a really rough shape. The irrigation ditches were all filled up, the flumes had all rotted away, and the fields all covered with a rank growth of Russian thistle. It called for a lot of work and effort, and we asked our Uncle Bill if he would try and undertake to put this ranch back in shape again.

Bill scratched his old grizzled head — he was a little past sixty years young then — and said he'd do his best. When Uncle Bill said that, I sure knew he would do just that. The operations started again almost from scratch, as it had to have new flumes, ditches all cleaned out, and the fields ploughed up. It meant a lot of work for Bill and two or three other boys I sent down there to help him. Bill put in a big garden that year, as pretty near anything grows on that Fraser River, as long as you have water to irrigate, but the weeds are an awful problem to battle with.

Bill got old Henry Hinck to irrigate and look after the garden, but he said Henry was so slow that the weeds got so far ahead of him and his hoe, by the time he had finished hoeing one row, the weeds at the top end of the row had started all over again, so the garden was not much of a success that summer. I always found that a small garden well looked after was better than a big garden just chock full of weeds. I have always given Uncle Bill the full credit for bringing that place back to production.

There was not a great deal of social life in that Big Bar country for the young folks growing up, and in the early 1920's an effort was made by the settlers, and a log building was put up with the object of having some sort of a Community Hall. In the hall there were dances, church services for any kind of religious faith, and also for political meetings whenever the local candidate decided to come out and meet the settlers for a rare visit. On provincial or federal election days it was used as a voting centre for the folks around there.

The dances were more or less always colourful affairs, lively and full of ginger and snap amongst the young folks. Many of the Big Bar boys were natural-born fiddlers, and the girls were all darn good dancers. The sight of these good-looking half-breed gals all tucked out in smart Timothy Eaton dresses with their hair all decorated up with bright coloured ribbons, just looked like water in the desert to an active snoozer of a half-lonesome cowboy. Many romances were started, and some finished, around that Community Hall. Just outside the hall were some thick willows and cottonwood trees, right close to the creek and these provided an all-out setting, so necessary and important, to the privacy required for successful courting. One of the local boys must have been reading some of Bill Shakespeare's plays at some time, as he christened this quiet little spot "The Bridge of Sighs."

There was little or none of real ready cash in the Big Bar country and the boys couldn't afford to buy hard liquor of any kind, so they got around by making their own brews of very stout moonshine. This Mountain Dew was made of yeast cakes, potatoes, raisins and sugar, sometimes laced up with lemon extract flavouring. This mixture being strong and packing quite a wallop to it, made the boys just as drunk and carefree as the real genuine liquor would, so there was always an odd fight or two and a real honest-to-God top-hand row at most of their dances.

The local police authorities in Clinton used to show up on the creek every so often, and sometimes around these dance nights, but they never accomplished any results to speak of. The Big Bar moonshiners were a pretty tight-knitted outfit, and the Masonic Lodge had nothing on them when it came to being secret.

I remember at one time (the boys told me afterwards about it) that the local "bull" from Clinton arrived around midnight at one of their dances. He parked his car right on top of a cache of three crocks of moonshine covered with leaves and dirt, which, of course, stayed there until after the lawman headed back for Clinton, and needless to say the boys got quite a kick out of that.

The fact of so many rows, quarrels and fights at the dances gave the Community Hall a darned poor reputation all through the South Cariboo, and one of the boys christened the hall The Howling Dog Dance Hall and the name has stuck with it to this day.

I think I was at two of these dances in my time. It was over nine miles from the main O K to the Howling Dog, and my days were too full to care about dancing. I did drive or ride up to the lake two or three times a month and I'd always take in a dance at the lake to help Peg out in entertaining her guests. Of course, there were no rowdy drunks and fights at the lake dances which were different entirely from the wild fandangos on the creek at the Howling Dog Hall. I guess young folks had to have some fun and frolics, and the Howling Dog was the only place they had to gather together in.

I was at one Anglican Church service at the hall which was attended by a mixed gathering of all religions, and the Bishop of Cariboo, a gentleman called The Right Reverend Bishop Fred Wells, preached with great sincerity. He stayed overnight with me at the O K Ranch after the service.

When we'd had a real good supper, the Bishop and I were talking in our sitting room on many matters, with me free and easy cowboy style. I was not much of a model for the English grammar, and after talking on many different kinds of topics the bishop kind of startled me by suddenly asking me, "Mr. Marriott, would you mind doing me a favour?" To which I replied, "Yes, I'd do you a favour any old time," figuring that the bishop was probably going to tap me for a few bucks for the grand old Church. However, he remarked to me, "I wish you would refrain from using the good Lord's name with such easy flippancy." Believe me, this sure did set this old cowboy right back on his haunches, so to speak. I hastened to explain to the Bishop that a lot of our so-called bad language was always said with a smile, and really meant no wrong of any kind. However, I took the lesson to heart a little, and tried not to break out in bad language as much, except I know that on certain times if I got really riled up, the plain modest talk was entirely forgotten for awhile. I never had much time for milk and lemonade expressions like "Oh, bother," or "dash it all." They never seemed to let off much steam, but just the same, I figured Bishop Wells was a fine character and had a very well balanced approach to all the human trials and weaknesses. I felt real privileged to meet him, that sort of preacher. If he didn't do you any good, he sure as hell wouldn't do you any harm.

In the late thirties and in the earlier depression days, there was quite an assortment of gold miners along that Fraser River at Big Bar and there remained a few of them, shovelling gravel into a home-made Long Tom sluice box, maybe getting from a dollar and a half to four dollars a day in the two months of low water along the river. These prospecting boys were all of them confident that some day they'd strike it rich the great tomorrow, or the next day or the day after, and their great hope that some day they'd make a real win was the only thing that kept them going. Among these prospectors were five characters that are very worthy of remembrance. Their names were Bill Trimble, Porcupine Bill, Dick Butler, Davey Jones and Jim Fletcher.

Bill Trimble was by far the most able and well-posted prospector that ever dug holes and turned over rocks in the Big Bar country. He told me that in fourteen years of placering at the head of Watson Bar Creek on the west side of the Fraser, he had taken out over twenty-eight thousand dollars worth of gold, and I believe that Bill had far less of the campfire pipe dreams than most prospectors are afflicted with. He always carried one or two strychnine pills in a little glass bottle in his shirt pocket when he was out prospecting and alone in the hills. He observed to me that if a rock slide or some other calamity hit him, rather than suffer a slow death in pain, he could always make a quick out with the pills.

Porcupine Bill, as he was nicknamed — I never did hear of him by his right name — was a short, thick-set old chap with a long straggling beard that swept the top button of his overalls. A man who never worried a day in his life — always an optimist with a friendly howdy when he saw you. He had more patches sewn on his shirt and overalls than old Jacob had colours in his shirt, and he lived in a dirty dugout along the river. When he would crawl out of his dugout to see you it kind of reminded me, somehow, of an old bear coming out of his den in the spring. I think he got his name — Porcupine Bill — from the fact that he had eaten a lot of porcupine when he was on his trips to the mountains. The porcupine is always a slow-travelling little fellow and easy killed with a stick. Bill was a great rugged type of fellow, and would not take help from anyone. He stayed that way, even when he was dying.

Dick Butler was a very up-and-coming sort of fellow, and would turn his hand to any kind of work until such times as he had enough ahead to get himself another grub-stake, and away he'd go on another trip looking for that elusive gold either along the river or up in the high mountain west of Big Bar.

One spring, Dick arrived at the Big Bar ferry with a pack on his back and a young fellow with him, and he assured me that he had it made on this trip, and pointed to a couple of good empty sacks he had with him, telling me that the extra sacks were to pack the gold in, when he returned from the mountains.

I didn't run on to Dick Butler for around two months, and when I asked him how the gold turned out, he turned his snappy brown eyes to me and said, "You know, Harry, I'd have done all right if that young fellow had been any good." So I asked Dick what was wrong with the young fellow. He looked like a skookum young lad to me. Dick replied, "Well, we were only out of grub four days and here's this young fellow just a belly-aching to beat hell." Dick always had a good out, and a top-hand excuse for all his mining disappointments, but after he received his old age pension he moved to Clinton and was considered the unofficial mayor and story teller of the town.

The old Welshman, Davey Jones, was a wise old character. A jack-of-all-trades, but a master of none, he lived in a cabin about four miles from the main O K Ranch, and every June for over twenty-five years Davey would strike out prospecting in the mountains west of the Fraser, riding a gentle saddle horse and leading a pack horse loaded with his grub, blankets, frypan, axe, shovel and miner's pick.

He would come to me at the O K every year in the spring, and tell me he knew for sure where he'd find it that year, and if I'd just put a little in the grub-stake for him, he'd stake me a claim, and I'd be on the road to riches for sure, so for years I would dig up ten to thirty dollars each time, for Davey's annual trip to the hills. Nothing very worthwhile came from any of Davey's trips out there in the mountains and I sometimes wondered if Davey wasn't taking some sort of vacation out there, and not seriously looking for any minerals. I remember old Grant Lee telling me in his Texas drawl, "Well, Harry, I ain't got much money, but if I did have any, I wouldn't let that fellow have it to go out to those mountains and stand around a campfire, tromping the grass flat, and just awarming his ass on the campfire, with my money." However, I always gave old Davey the benefit of the doubt and finally after grub-staking him to the tune of four hundred dollars, spread over a long period of years, I finally decided to quit, and let the gold stay where it was.

I knew another very persistent old fellow, a Boer War veteran named Jim Fletcher, who dug a tunnel in a clay and gravel bank at least fifty feet above the river, and after about two summers' work took out some real coarse gold nuggets that were sure pretty to see. Along came two Vancouver engineers and purchased his claim for quite a nice little cheque. These two Vancouver boys took out over eight thousand dollars in gold in a little space not over ten feet wide and twenty-odd feet long, but they ran out of that little pocket and despite all the digging and channelling efforts they did, they could find no more gold in that claim.

The gold along the Fraser was mostly in very fine particles known as flour gold. In washing out the gravel through the Long Tom sluice box, a lot of care had to be taken so that these fine particles of gold didn't carry on through the box and out on to the dump. To offset this, most of the boys used to have a piece of woollen blanket at the lower end of the sluice box. This way the flour gold would be saved by sticking to the piece of blanket.

It seemed to me the gold was found in little pockets in the rocks, sand and gravel, as I have seen prospectors find a streak for a day or two, then go for days on end without getting any gold. All in all, I think there are probably still millions more in gold along that Fraser River, but there is sure a big pile of gravel and rocks mixed up with it.

In my years I have seen three different outfits come into this Big Bar country with high-priced gold mining equipment, and leave with no return to speak of for their time or money. However, there always was, and always will be, a distinct fascination in looking for gold.

A gold bug fever is very hard to get rid of, and out of your system, but there never was a more truthful saying than "Gold is where you find it," and that's just exactly where it is.

Chapter 15

Famous Folks from the Coast

MEANWHILE ON THE O K Ranch headquarters, we were hitting along on all cylinders and doing our darndest to get the best results for the least amount of money being spent out. Our meat business to Bralorne Mines and our short-order business in Clinton and way points along the P.G.E. railway taking the main spotlight on our operation, and followed up by the busy session with guests and fishing folks at the lake in the summer months.

Our old stand-by, Uncle Bill, was really doing a land office job at the river, in growing us a pretty good supply of real good spuds, some fruit and a lot of sugar beets which were used to feed our hogs, brood sows mostly, in the winter time.

The fall came along and winter set in again with not so much snow, but a lot of cold weather showed up. Mr. Harrison happened to be up on one of his frequent trips to the ranch, and after a little fall of snow it turned kind of cold — going down to around twenty-five below zero. During his stay the motor burnt out one night in our pump house and that put the pump out of action. That put us really in a spot as pretty well everything was geared to run by electric power from the hydro Pelton water wheel we had on the ranch. There was nothing to be done about it except send the motor down to Vancouver to get it re-wound and tuned up so I decided to ride to Kelly Lake that evening and lead a pack horse, with the motor tied down solid on the pack saddle. Mr. Harrison decided he'd go back to Vancouver by the P.G.E. too, so we saddled up a horse for him and we both started off around two o'clock in the afternoon, both of us with plenty of good winter clothes on.

Well, sir, we could not trot along with this pack horse, leading him with a pack on, so we walked our horses along as fast as we could and when we got to Eleven Mile Creek, it was getting dark and I could feel it getting a lot colder, probably nearly thirty below anyway. There was a little cabin below the road at Eleven Mile Creek, and I saw a small light shining through a very small window. I asked Mr. Harrison if he'd like to get off his horse for a few minutes and get warmed up. He said he thought it might be a good idea. When we went to the cabin door it was opened by Tim Haller, who was Gussie Haller's boy, and it appears that Tim was camped there, trying to trap a few squirrels. One look around the dingy cabin showed me that Tim was having pretty tough sledding. His supper, which he was cooking, was made up of a hellish strong brew of black coffee and no sugar or milk, and some tough-looking dough dodgers made with flour and water, but the real titbit was fried squirrel in a frypan on the stove.

Tim allowed he didn't have much to offer, but if we wanted any to fly right at it. We tried out a little nibble at the fried squirrel, of which he had three or four in the pan, and having got warmed up good with a drink of that coffee, so strong it would have floated a full-sized ship, we started out for the last fifteen miles to Kelly Lake.

I said to Mr. Harrison as we were riding along — the stars blinking and winking at us by this time — "How did you like that tenderloin on that fried squirrel, George?" Mr. Harrison allowed that while the steak didn't choke him at all, he thought that it was a real good Samaritan turn that Tim offered us, and there's no doubt that Tim did his best for us.

Poor Tim had trapped seven squirrels that day for which he got ten cents a head — skinned and stretched on a board at that — and I guess it must have kept him scratching to make it go.

We got down to Kelly Lake where Mr. Harrison took the train to Vancouver, and next morning after a good breakfast at Bill Birdsell's, I stepped up on my horse and, leading the other two horses, I headed for home.

The green grass came again in 1938 springtime and found me in the usual busy run of ranch activity. The ball always had to be kept rolling in our efforts — crops to put in on Big Bar Mountain, cows to run out on the ranch and every Saturday, and sometimes Sundays, were big days for me in our ranch slaughterhouse. I had to kill three and sometimes four head of beef every week and in addition, four fat hogs every week from fall till the end of May each year. I sure took a great pride in my butchering efforts. My slaughterhouse and meat cooler were always spotlessly clean and our meat turned out well wrapped, and the ranch developed a real good reputation.

Mr. Harrison took intense interest in everything that was going on. Sometimes he'd bring some of his personal friends up from Vancouver with him. Through him I became acquainted with several of the most successful business people in Canada and the coast country. These folks were always pleased to get a change from their day-to-day rush of city life. Amongst those I can remember being at the old O K were my old C.O. of army days and an old friend, "the Honourable Jack Roaf," and Mr. Morton who was one of the head managers for the Canadian Bank of Commerce, who came on a short visit with the great industrialist, Mr. H. R. MacMillan, whose name as a great timber magnate was famous all over Canada, the U.S.A. and Great Britain. I shall always remember the forceful power of concentration and the quiet decisive manner, and well-chosen words that he used in conversation. I mentally figured that it would take a pretty good man to follow along in his tracks.

General A. D. MacRae, who was one of our tops in World War I days, came. So did the big tycoon, Major Austin Taylor of Bralorne Mines, and Mr. Gorden Farrell who was president of the B.C. Telephone Company, and a great agriculturist named Mr. Pete Moore, who was the manager of the government farms in British Columbia.

We had good hay crops on the ranch that year, but on our dry farm efforts on Big Bar Mountain we could not say as much. Things were not any worthwhile good that year, as the returns you'd get were on the new dollar for an old dollar basis, which, while it don't win you anything, don't lose either, but the expenses paid out in growing those dry farm crops rolled up pretty high and you had to have grain enough to offset the overhead expenses.

I picked up another good all-round man that year named Bill MacDonald, who hailed from New Westminster. He was always ready to give a hand, even on Sundays, and he was a great companion for my thirteen-year-old boy, Ronnie, who rode a cayuse every day four miles up and back to a little log schoolhouse. Ronnie, like all other kids in this area, had a great ambition to become a real cowboy. The Big Bar country produced a lot of real good boys on a horse, which was quite natural, as the saddle horse is and always will be the most important function in the handling of a cow ranch.

We had a very good winter in 1938, with not too much snow and cold weather spells, which was a whole lot easier on our hay stacks. It is always a very nice feeling to have a little extra hay left over in any spring. In early March I got another small brainwave with an idea to increase our yearly ranch take-in. When Mr. Harrison came up on his next trip I put it up to him for us to go into the turkey business in a small way first, as I knew that turkeys did real well in our country after they had got six weeks or so of age on them. The result was that Mr. Harrison made a deal with a turkey-hatching farmer in the Aldergrove area of the Chilliwack valley. This farmer agreed to produce us three hundred young turkeys which we would take at six weeks old. These young turkeys were all incubated birds, and a far better bet than turkeys hatched out from under the old mother hen, because the young turkeys raised up by the mother were always a lot wilder. The incubated birds, however, always stuck around fairly close to where they were fed, and as long as they had feed, fresh water and a little good clear, clean ground to run over, with a bit of green feed handy, they did all right.

Turkeys up to six weeks old are very touchy and delicate birds to raise. Cold days in spring and wet rainy weather, and cold nights will certainly be the cause of a good many casualties. I always found that after six weeks old, they took on a considerable degree of hardiness and given any kind of a break from that age on the turkey will grow, put on weight and turn out to be a real fine bird.

I fixed up an old hay shed close to the O K buildings and put chicken wire all around it and tar paper for ten feet high around the whole hay shed so as to keep out the wind and the draughts, and put up two-by-four lumber for roosts, nailed with the flat side up. The reason for this was that a turkey roosting on a round pole has a tendency to acquire a crooked breast bone.

We had to pay more for the young turkeys at six weeks old than as day-old chicks but it was well worth it to us. The O K Ranch being nearly thirty-five hundred feet high, the nights are always cool and we had no accommodation for any day-old chicks at all. The young six-week-old turkeys arrived in our ranch truck around the end of May and for the first few nights I had an all-night job keeping these young fellows on their roosts because they would get chilly in the night air, jump off their roosts and huddle up together for warmth.

I had two lanterns lit in the hay shed and would pick up the young birds and put them back on their roosts again. I knew all along that if I didn't break up that huddle the young fellows inside would surely all smother to death from lack of air. It took me about four nights of constant watching all night, and from then on the birds stayed on their roosts. Every night just before they hopped up on their roosts we fed them whole wheat, as that gave the turkeys something in their stomachs to grind on and in that way they got internal heat. At that time we were milking three cows on the ranch and the skim milk was a great asset to their daily feed.

I had a lot of worry and effort to find a man willing enough to take an intelligent interest in looking after our hogs and turkeys and milking the cows. The choreman is a pretty important fellow around a mixed farm. His work calls for a day-by-day steady round of routine, Sundays and holidays included, and it was the factor of every day eternally on the grindstone that contributed to the distaste the average man had for being the choreman.

I tried out a lot of them and had to get rid of most, but I did have three real good choremen — as long as they lasted. One, named Stanley Macallan, was a world beater, except that on two occasions he went out on a big drunk for two or three days and I just had to let him go. I always prided myself on being a real early morning riser and was surprised to find that Stanley was always up ahead of me. I finally found out that he had been gassed up some in the World War I fracas and had to sleep with his head high up on plenty of pillows so as not to wake up choking, so I guess he slept pretty light.

I had another boy called Walter Tomlinson, who was a good capable all-round fellow. He saved every dollar of his wages, and after two years decided to quit and try and do something for himself. I was certainly sorry to see him pull out as Walter was all man at any and all times.

The last good choreman I had was a very likeable Irishman named John Close, who was a faithful fellow for over two years, and remained so until he became very much in love with a local lady. As he could not brush himself away from the lady's chains, which interfered a great deal with the ever-important matter of tending to our hogs, turkeys and milk cows, I finally had to let him go. From then on I never did have any regular choreman, but Ronnie used to help out in doing a lot after school hours.

I took most of our brood sows and their litters down to Uncle Bill on the river ranch and they did very well, getting a little grain every day and scampering around in a little orchard below the buildings and picking up every windfall apple that ever fell. After the hay crops were taken off, they would get a considerable run on the alfalfa fields. All of them had to have their snouts full of hog rings to keep them from rooting up the hay fields and the only hogs I kept up at the O K headquarters were those that I penned up and fed till they were six months old, or close to it, then they made their exit through our slaughterhouse door.

We had quite a bit of rain at the right time in the summer of 1939 and our hay crops were really good that year also. This meant that we had a good dry farm crop on the mountain which was sure a real benefit to the ranch.

Along in September I was in our slaughterhouse at the ranch taking the hide off one of our steers for the Bralorne business when a neighbour and old-time friend, Harry Coldwell, of the Jesmond store and post office, passed by. As he came to the meat house window he told me that the French and British had declared war on the aggressive followers of the Adolf Hitler fanatic in Germany. This being followed by our beloved Canada as well, who was by far and large the most important member of the British Nations Club.

Of course, "once a soldier, generally always a soldier," is a very true saying and I was very disturbed. I pondered on the far-reaching consequences that another world war upheaval would bring. I knew that I was not too far from being fifty years old and any attempt of mine towards joining the armed forces would only result in a firm but kindly refusal. On top of that I was the practical king pin in quite an operation and I would not consider making any hardship for my old-time associate, Mr. Harrison.

Around the first week in November I separated all the turkey hens from our flock and fed them entirely separate from the gobbler boys. The answer to that was that the gobblers, with no hens around to strut and show how good they were, turned their minds on eating and getting fat instead of this Romeo and Juliet game. The result was that they put on at least another three or four pounds in their last six weeks of feeding.

The problem of getting our turkeys marketed engaged a lot of my spare mental attention and when Mr. Harrison came up on his next visit, he and I both had serious pow-wows as to how to get the best disposal and price for our turkeys. I suggested that, above all things, we must make an effort to keep these turkeys from getting into the meat packers' hands, because the packers would get a far greater ratio of profit than they were entitled to for doing very little except passing the dressed turkey over to a retail butcher shop. In turn the retail shop would just take the turkey off a hook behind the counter, weigh and wrap it up for a customer, while we with our long hard efforts of raising, feeding and dressing out our turkeys, would only get a very small margin of profit from them. This looked just like it was — a plumb rotten deal for us after having borne all the burden, and the heat and toil of the day in raising them.

I said to Mr. Harrison, that as he was a member of the famous Vancouver Club and also conversant with most of the large-sized businessmen, and well-to-do folks down there, it looked to me that if he would get in touch with his friends and see if they would buy real top grain-fed and milk-fed turkeys raised right on the O K

Ranch in the Big Bar country, these fine birds with never a mean thought in their heads could be delivered right to their homes in Vancuover about three days before Christmas.

Mr. Harrison, my old guide, friend and philosopher, was much impressed by the idea. He made a list of many of his Vancouver friends and wrote each one a letter on the matter and pretty soon the orders came in for over a hundred and twenty dressed turkeys. I was a very great booster on this idea of finding your own market and customer as I have always been a strong advocate for the farmers and ranchers to own their own co-operative plants and processing units and to sell direct to John Jones, the customer. That way of direct selling is a method of cutting out that greedy middleman that thrived, wore a derby hat, fancy creased pants and probably patent leather shoes, and drove a big car with all the trimmings on it, on the long hard hours of blood, sweat and tears of the farmer who produced the initial product. It was taking all the cream off the bucket and just leaving the rancher the skim milk for his efforts.

I had very successfully tried to overcome this in creating our little dressed meat game for the Bralorne Mines and the thirty-odd other customers, and I failed to see any reason why the same principles could not be applied to all our agricultural products — right clean across Canada.

I know that a dressed beef carcass used to make us about fifteen dollars per head more than if we had sold the same cattle on a live-weight basis. On top of that we had the sale of well-salted hides and some carcass by-products to boil up for hog feed. It is a matter which should be first and foremost in the minds of all ranchers, as I know beyond all question of doubt that if I, a small pebble in the economic picture, could accomplish this it could certainly be done in a provincial or a national effort on the part of all farm producers. Nothing in life is ever done without enthusiasm, and that goes for everything from riding a bucking horse all the way up to courting and winning a nice girl.

I contacted our friends at the Bralorne Mines and all our beef customers around Clinton, so with the exception of a few which had to be sent to a meat packer in Vancouver, we managed to sell our turkeys on a direct order basis. The meat packer company "most generously" paid us twenty cents per pound for the turkeys and the same turkeys found their way to store counters and were sold to customers for forty and forty-three cents per pound — with little or not much effort involved in the deal.

Well, sir, the zero hour arrived and we had to kill those wonderful birds for market. I was sure proud of this flock. We started butchering these turkeys around the fifteenth of December. With three of us killing and taking off feathers, and three of us in the big kitchen in the O K cook-house — Peg being there herself and helping out to beat hell, by carefully going over each turkey, taking off little pin feathers, washing their feet and scrubbing their claws, wiping their heads and wrapping the heads in paper and setting their wings and feet in the correct position. These grand turkeys looked exactly like they were — royal birds — and all of us at the O K were real pleased with the job we had done on them.

We sent a pretty fair-sized bunch to our good friends at Bralorne, and the last best one hundred and twenty turkeys were weighed up and labelled to the Vancouver customers. Bill MacDonald and I took them down in the ranch truck over the highway to Vancouver — Bill stopping off at Westminster to see his folks. I must say that I was under quite a high tension, driving that truck into Vancouver, and I stalled around quite a bit until it was away late, figuring that there would be not too much traffic on the big Burrard Street at two o'clock in the morning.

I was just a country boy, never scared very often in driving a truck over our mountain roads in our Cariboo, but that is a far different game than driving around a big city. While I was sure that I was not going to run into anybody, I was kind of anxious that perhaps somebody might run me down instead. I finally reached Mr. Harrison's house on Cedar Crescent and taking the key out of the truck, I went up to the house, tip-toed through the back door, and went to sleep on his sofa in his big sitting room. No one heard me and they were surprised to find me when they came downstairs in the morning.

The next day, Mr. Harrison and I, with the help of an express man, delivered the dressed turkeys to the residential homes to which they had been ordered, and to each of these customers that I personally contacted, I expressed my thanks, and pleasure, in being privileged to bring them such a fine turkey. In many instances I told the head of the house, "When you've had a real good feed of turkey on Christmas Day, and you're setting back in your easy chair smoking a big fat cigar, what better thought could you have than the fact that by buying our good turkey, you have helped a hard-working outfit to pay up their bills and obligations." I figure that was a real worthy thought to have on Christmas Day.

They went over very well, and no complaints of any kind at all. After loading up the truck with cattle salt and ranch supplies I started back up the long trail to the O K Ranch, which took me a very long day, arriving home on Christmas Eve — just the right spot to be on a night like that.

On the trip home, I had to cross a very busy section at Granville and Georgia Streets and my truck stalled right in the middle of this busy intersection. I got started again and a big burly policeman roared out to me, "Where the hell do you think you're going, mon?" I hollered back, "I'm heading for the Cariboo." He said, "For Christ's sake, get to hell out of here then." I needed no second invitation, but I did just that and was real glad when I had passed over the big bridge at Westminster.

We averaged around forty-two cents a pound for our turkey effort to city customers which was quite a big difference from the miserable titbit of twenty cents a pound for a dressed turkey given us by that "generous" meat packing concern.

All those turkey customers, except one, paid for their turkeys. This one happened to be a great friend of Mr. Harrison and I mentioned this to him. George said to me, "Well, Harry, this boy is quite a friend of mine and I'll pay the O K Ranching Company for the two turkeys he got from the ranch." So I said, "That being the case, Mr. Harrison, I don't see why you should dig up for the turkeys; how would it be if we forget about it?" Which we did. Mr. Harrison was always an optimist and liked to look on the bright side of things and sometimes when something would hit us out of line, he had a great saying, "Well, Harry, it will be all the same a hundred years from now, won't it?"

Each winter for a matter of two weeks, generally in February, I would go down to Vancouver and take all the previous year's receipts and paid outs with me — in the shape of cheques taken in and paid out for the year. It was an account of my stewardship to Mr. Harrison and I stayed at his house as his guest while I was in Vancouver. Mr. Harrison had a fine charactered wife and two daughters and a son. They were Katherine and Nora and George, named after his dad. Kay, as her dad called her, was a brilliant type of girl, a natural born artist who in after years married a very successful young doctor.

George Junior was a mining and civil engineer with a great mathematical mind, just a figuring machine and a real brainy young man. Nonie, as her dad called Nora, was a very quiet and reserved type of girl and a studious, literary type. A truly wonderful gal who seemed like to me a real Christian kind of person that a fellow like myself only ever hears of once in a great while. I shall never forget as long as I am a breathing any breath, the kindness and the great hospitality shown to me by that warm-hearted, fine and friendly family. I grew to look on Mr. Harrison just like a boy looks towards his father. Even now, when he has long gone over that Big High Mountain I find myself missing him to beat hell.

For three years, young George stayed with me at the O K Ranch and helped me very largely in the running of the operation. His brains and ability were worth far more than the ranch could ever afford to pay. He left the ranch after getting married to a very attractive girl named Doris Browne, whose father was a very well-known eye specialist in Vancouver, and after returning down below to the coast, young George became actively interested in a large machinery enterprise.

I repeated the performance with turkeys in the late fall and Christmas of 1940, but had to forget about it after that time because all through 1940 things began to get a lot more difficult in the line of help. The war effort of our country intensified and it looked like a very grim period to me. The British were being bombed day and night by Goering's Air Force, and the French folded right up into a state of general collapse and just couldn't take it. Here at the O K Ranch four of our boys decided to join the armed forces and were accepted. The only real young man I had left was Edwin Loring who had tried twice to join up, each time coming back madder than a hornet. They had turned him down because he had a growth of bone in his nose which called for continual mouth breathing. Edwin was much disgusted over this, but like a lot more things in life, it couldn't be helped.

Our boys at the ranch, Bill MacDonald, Joe Murdoch, Jimmie Grinder and Bill Craig all left towards the spring of 1941. Bill MacDonald told me he really didn't want to go as his dad had told him a whole lot about World War I and what he went through, but Bill figured it was absolutely up to him to go. I woke up to the fact that I had lost these good lads and I'd have to get along the best I could and depend on older men to help run the ranch.

My boy, Ronnie, was not quite sixteen then, but he had left school and was busy helping out at the ranch. Mostly he was riding for the cattle on the range and in the pastures on the Big Bar Mountain. All needed quite a bit of riding around and keeping track of.

Uncle Bill down on the river had his hands full and was always short-handed. For a man of his age he really did wade through a lot of work. Edwin Loring was at the lake helping Peg, who was eternally trying to keep the ball rolling. Ronnie and myself, with two older men, were at the main O K headquarters.

In that year we rented the Crow's Bar pasture from the Gang Ranch which was the layout where I had put in around four years in the days of 1913. Having that winter range at our disposal, we were able to winter a lot of cattle without feeding them any hay, which surely was a big help to us. That Crow's Bar winter range was a great asset to anyone in the cow business. The summer of 1941 I had a little over two hundred cows and calves in that upper part of the Crow's Bar pasture. They were all branded that year in the big corral below the cabin. My boy, Ronnie, who was a good roper then, would rope the calves on a hind leg and take a turn on his saddle horn and head for the branding fire. I always castrated the bull calves myself, as I figured it was a top job to avoid infection, and I'd get Uncle Bill to brand them. Those branding days were lots of fun. A rancher never gets tired of seeing his brand and earmark on a lot of good husky well-bred calves. Good calf crops are an absolute must to any rancher if he wants to stay in the cow business.

With the war on, any active men who were not in the armed forces, were working in munition plants and war factories, so I redoubled my efforts to keep things going, and from daylight to dark I was sure agoing like a cat shot in the ass with a boot-jack.

That summer we had another dry season with fair crops on anything we were irrigating, but the dry farm crops were a hopeless failure, with not even enough grain to cover a third of their expense.

At this time most of the homesteaders on Big Bar Mountain had pulled out of the area, just beaten right out for lack of enough rain. The company bought out several of their holdings and there were only two or three left. One of them was a rugged old character named Miles Clinke, who was a man of real tough calibre. Miles had a few head of cattle on the mountain, and he'd be out riding along in the snow with a black cowboy hat on his head and cowboy boots on. On real cold days, if I happened to meet him out riding, his lips might be just aquivering with the cold, but the tough old bluffer would say, "God, it's sure nice to be out on such a warm day."

Miles pulled all his own teeth out as they loosened in his head with pyorrhea, with the exception of the last one. He had to have a little help with that grinder, as he needed someone to take a stout cinch hold on his head, while he tugged away with an old pair of pliers.

A few weeks later he read an "ad" in a Prairie paper, telling how they would send him a bunch of wax and when he got the wax he got some sort of impression on his gums and sent them away to Winnipeg for a set of false teeth, which arrived by the mail. Miles Clinke was the only man I have ever known who could chew tobacco in a church service without spitting. It is quite an art. I tried it once in my young years without any success. I saw Miles, on the one and only occasion I was at Divine Service at the Howling Dog Dance Hall, when Bishop Wells held the service there and this resourceful old cowboy sat through the whole service complacently chewing his cud of tobacco without spitting once, and with a look of complete content on his face.

In the fall of 1941 I purchased quite a number of pretty fair cows, and some replacement steers, and a real fine bunch of heifer calves. These were loaded on the P.G.E. at Williams Lake and shipped down to the 59 Mile at the Chasm and somehow or other I got hold of a couple of fellows to help me drive them to the O K Ranch. It was the last time I ever bought cattle in any quantity, outside of an odd few head here and there from local sources.

That year, I bought another small wild hay meadow up Big Bar Creek from the ranch and near the head of Little Bar Lake. It had a very old cabin and tumble-down barn on it, and the fences were all down flat, but we cut some wild hay on it, and moved up some cows there that winter. One of the older men I had at the home ranch moved up and camped in the old cabin. It was full of mice and there were big cracks between the logs where the dirt and moss had fallen out, letting lots of daylight and cold frosty air into the cabin.

I meditated on this some and decided I would try and remedy the situation, so we fed the cows from the team and sleigh just outside the cabin and when the load of hay was thrown off I'd stand around with an old shovel and I'd wait till I saw an old cow lift up her tail, and then I'd shovel up some of that hot fresh manure and I'd run up to the cabin and throw the hot stuff right at a crack in the cabin with Babe Ruth accuracy. The result was that the fresh manure froze in a matter of a few minutes. In a day or so, all the cracks were sealed off plumb tight and the cabin got so warm that sometimes the door would have to be left wide open to let the inside cool down a little. The idea sure worked out real good. Years of living in our old Cariboo and having to deal with, and survive in, many situations will certainly make a very handy snoozer of a man at most things.

Chapter 16

Ranching on the Wrong Side of Fifty

TIME AND TIDE wait for no man and 1942 came tearing around the corner and found me faced with several problems, which, of course, I had to talk over with the "old General," as I affectionately referred to Mr. Harrison. We decided that we would completely forget about our dry farm efforts on Big Bar Mountain, because in the period of eight years we had had two top-hand crops, three crops of breaking even by just getting the new dollar for the old dollar and three years of total failure. We quit putting in any more dry farm crops and hoped that eventually there would be some sort of grass coverage grow back again on those acres we had cultivated for eight years with such darned small success. From that time on we bought all the grain that was ever used for feeding purposes.

The grain was shipped in from the prairie provinces where the good Lord most always sends them enough rain. It was expensive, as the freight costs were high and getting higher but at least we did have one advantage. If we spent a thousand dollars buying grain we had the grain anyway, and it was better to buy than to spend time, wages, gas, oil, horse-work on our teams and so on putting in crops on that mountain, and maybe never getting any crop.

Hindsight and looking back through the game of life is of not much value to any of us, except for reference, but all through the years it had certainly proved that the Big Bar Mountain area should never have had a plough stuck into the soil, in the original start off. The final outcome was just nothing but a headache and a heartache for those who put in all those hard, long and disappointing hours.

Uncle Bill down on the river really did a first-class job of raising us a lot of alfalfa hay that year. The old boy was just tireless and I'd told him, "Bill, old-timer, I don't see how you can go through so darned much work and get away with it." Uncle Bill twisted his grand old face around, and said, "I'm going to live a long while, just as my old grandma in Ireland did. She lived to be one hundred and three and she wouldn't have died then if she hadn't bit off too big a chew of Irish plug tobacco and choked herself to death." Such was the calibre and the tough gut that made up this fine old Irish hombre.

The strain and stress of trying to keep our meat business going, as well as trying to run a scattered ranch, began to tell on me quite a bit. I had turned past fifty years and each week I had to spend at least two days or more in our meat-house — butchering our weekly supply of beef and dressed hogs. I had no one, that I could rely on, to do this but myself. Union wage butchers were just out of the question. I didn't have enough steady work in our meat business to keep a man at it six days a week, and it was not a job for amateurs. I had no choreman to help me out in the many details around the ranch, and it just turned out to be an eternal grind for me to keep all things on the move and looked after. In 1942 there were only four days in the whole year that I didn't work, and I was sure getting tired.

After a lot of real thinking and studying on the matter I asked Mr. Harrison if it would be agreeable with him if we decided to wind up our butchering activities and return to selling our cattle and hogs by live weight. In the meantime our government at Ottawa had clamped down a ceiling price on our dressed beef, but our costs of all things connected with the game continued to keep rising. Although the government came along some time later with wage ceilings and other moves to keep costs down, I don't think that they were well adhered to.

Mr. Harrison and I were sure sorry to write finis on our business with Bralorne Mines. They were the finest outfit that I ever did business with. We sent them our last shipment around the eighth day of October 1942, after eight years of most friendly relationships and loyal service.

Meanwhile the war churned along with grim intensity and saw the United States become involved in Europe and in the Pacific. The frequent wallops in the rear that our boys got, were really rough for me to listen to over our ranch radio.

I remember how I was really madder than a wet hen when the news came that the super duper German battleship, *Bismark*, had lobbed a shell right down on the British battleship *Hood*. I said one day at dinner to two elderly fellows who were helping me, "If our boys get that *Bismark*, I'll give five dollars to the church." Sure enough, a week or so later the navy announced that they had sunk the *Bismark*, and I rejoiced and sent a five-dollar bill to the Anglican Church warden in Clinton, telling him how I had promised the good Lord a five spot for His church as a token of heartfelt thanks to Him for sending that *Bismark* and all hands to the bottom of the Atlantic. It evened up the score, and the church warden received the five bucks without any comments on his part.

In the tail end of January 1943, I went down to Vancouver with the year's statement of the "ins and outs," and, of course, stayed at Mr. Harrison's house enjoying the warm degree of friendship and kindness always shown me by that fine family. I had an odd, but kind of funny, experience while I was down in that coast country. A bunch of guests and visitors had arrived at the Harrison house for tea, bridge and social talk, and one of the visitors was a dignitary of the old Church of England. Mr. Harrison made me acquainted with this top-ranking sky pilot and I, of course, gave him the usual Canadian greeting of "Pleased to meet you, sir." This cake-fed mogul turned round to me and in his extra high Oxford accent, said, "Why are you so pleased to meet me?" This kind of took me back for a second as I figured this stranger was just trying to make a damn fool out of me in front of the others. I thought real fast for a second and said, "Well, sir, I've always been pleased to meet a headliner in any game and I do sure figure I'm a headliner in my game." I guess that showed His Reverence that this old Big Bar cowboy wasn't all hayseed and horse manure, and could maybe hold my end up with him any old day.

That winter, we received an offer from a well-built and quiet-speaking young man named Robert E. Cromie, a prominent member of the newspaper family. He wanted to buy the river holdings down on the Fraser. After a lot of heavy meditation, a sale of the river ranch was made to him and he moved up from Vancouver with his charming wife and two little kiddies. We became good neighbours and friends and in his first few years we were of help to him in the many details of the cow business in which, at that time, he had not acquired a great deal of experience. The Cromie's still own that river ranch today, and have proved themselves to be a great asset to that country.

The summer of that year saw us with a somewhat reduced operation. Uncle Bill came back home again to the main O K and helped us put up our hay crops. In early fall we proceeded to round up our beef cattle for shipping to the P.G.E. railroad at the Chasm and we were joined by Mr. Bob Cromie, who shipped his beef on the same drive with us.

We started out with several carloads from the O K Ranch and drove them fourteen miles the first day to Big Bar Lake, where we rested a day. We had lots of grass in the lake pasture for our beef to fill up on, and the following day we eased them along another ten miles to Beaver Dam Lake where we put up our tent and camped out close to the creek. Our beef grazed in a neighbour's pasture for the night. We all of us enjoyed a real big hot supper by the campfire and bedded down just as snug as an oyster in his shell.

In the morning rain apelted down like a Chinese monsoon, and we had a real wet trip into the 59 Mile that afternoon. We did have the benefit of a hot fire and a dry bed that night, and our beef were inside a pasture. The next morning was our shipping day and instead of coralling our beef in the yards, we waited, and held our herd on some good grass until one of us saw the beef buyer driving along the road. I had not been live-weight shipping for eight years, but I had not forgotten the old chiselling days of the early thirties, and the old poker-playing tactics of the packer buyers.

I told all the boys, "For God's sake handle these cattle as easy as you can getting them on the scales." If a beef gets riled up and excited in the stock-pens, he'll let go maybe two to five pounds of manure. That manure at live weight price — say eight cents a pound or more — let go in a yard before the steer is weighed — means about 20 to 30 cents each time. If you have fifty head and they all let go, it means you have lost fifteen to maybe twenty bucks or more. If the steers let go a bucket full after they were weighed that was no loss to our outfit. When you run into these tough chiselling buyers, it doesn't hurt a fellow a bit to try and figure up some wrinkles of his own to save a dollar.

We sold the beef and loaded them up, and started to ride back to our Beaver Dam camp, and doggoned if it didn't come pouring rain again and real hard all the way back to the camp. We sure had a wet supper that night, the pouring rain darned near put our campfire out. Bob Cromie proved that he could take it without hollering about it, just the same as the rest of us. We had quite a few rides and interchange of cowboy work with Mr. Cromie during the years and we always found Bob kept his end up the best he could in all details. Little by little he became one of the mountain men with the boys, which I mentally figured, was a real feather in his cap.

Chapter 17

War: Range Cattle vs. Horses

IT WAS IN THE YEAR OF 1943 that our range area and the ranchers in general became much closer in touch with the Provincial Forestry Department which controls all matters in regard to the government lands and the timber areas of our province. There was a special branch of the Lands and Forests devoted to handling the grazing areas.

For years the ranchers had, many of them, tried to organize cattlemen's associations in the Clinton, Big Bar and Gang Ranch areas. These associations always started out with a real bang up good start, but petering out after awhile through lack of energetic leadership. There had been two started in former years, both of them had faded out.

Nevertheless, another cattlemen's association was formed, with an objective of looking after the best interests of the range areas, and this time it looked to me that this one might be made to stick. I took quite an active part in this association, which was of considerable benefit to ranchers as it gave them a chance to speak collectively. While the Forestry Department always reserved the right to make any final decision on range matters, they listened and often reacted upon the ranchers' recommendations.

I found some of the range-land boys that had a lot of very valuable knowledge in relation to grass and grazing, passed it on to the ranchers, and many cattlemen were benefited a great deal by taking the advice of the experimental boys at their range grass station located a few miles out from the up-and-acoming cow town of Kamloops. Having met and compared ideas with quite a few of them, I would say that these boys were a well-posted bunch of students of the big outdoors and not all duds, or the pets of political patronage which is so often the case in government departments.

It has bothered me considerable as to why the ranchers and farmers have always been so backward and indifferent towards organization of any kind on a co-operative, or union, or association basis. So many of them would give lip service, but when it came to the actual stand together, final jump, they shied around it, like a cold-shouldered horse. I have often wondered if many of our ranchers are defeatists at heart, having been jammed around by the packers and middlemen, commission men and so on, for so long and so successfully, that they get an attitude that they are licked before they start. Every business I know of has some form of protective association except these ranchers and farmers who have only played around with the fringes of collective organization.

Some years ago I was a School Trustee for our South Cariboo area. At one meeting in Ashcroft, the School Board were confronted with three fast-talking, up-on-their-toes young men all doing a lot of real boosting to raise up the school teachers' wages. I listened to their harangue and asked one of them how they could expect higher wages when the ranchers, who paid at least 75 per cent of the school taxes, were in a price-cost squeeze and after their bills were paid had little or nothing for their work and investment.

Of course, this fell off the boys like water off a duck's back, and when I made some perhaps sarcastic remarks about their union, they objected to the word union being used and told me it was termed a federation. I replied, "You can call a pig house an emporium but it's still a hog pen just the same." However, the boys won out and got their raise with their collective effort and ultimatum — "More money for us or your schools may shut down, and your kids will run wild."

I have meditated some, as to what would happen if the ranchers and farmers were to go on strike same as the unions, or federations — no milk truck going to town, no car loads of beef, no train load of wheat, hogs, eggs or spuds, going in to any of the cities and town dwellers. I know that without grub to sustain existence the people wouldn't have the necessary strength to stagger to a toilet, and the only sound you'd hear in a couple of weeks would be the hollow sound of a carpenter's hammer, trying to make coffins. You can't eat ten-dollar bills — they'd make doggoned poor sustenance for a human being. Maybe at some stage the city dwellers might learn just how necessary the hard-working farmers and ranchers are for the preservation of human life and the country's economy.

Co-operative effort, owning their own plants and running and selling their own products through their own co-op stores is the only answer for successful marketing of farm products.

However much I have done or tried to do, I have always been like old John the Baptist crying in our economic wilderness, trying to get the boys to fully, finally and totally co-operate. I have been listened to in respectful silence but nothing much has been accomplished as yet.

The winter passed and the warm sun and Chinook winds made their annual appearance in March of 1944, the run-off snow filling up the lakes on the range and giving us the promise of plenty of water for irrigation. As usual when every spring came around, our Uncle Bill would tell me in his wise old way, "Harry, we made it again, and we've got two summers and one winter ahead of us now." We proceeded with our yearly spring work which was not quite the everlasting rush of other years when dry farm crops were put in and the meat business was going full swing.

We were very lucky in having a good reasonable winter, as we had quite a few cattle running on the famous old Crow's Bar winter range that we had rented from the Gang Ranch. I always tried my best to look after that strip good because grass on low elevations along that Fraser just meant that the cows could eat grass in winter, as against having hay thrown out to them with a pitch fork in the higher up snowball country.

All winter long every week, I'd ride over from the main O K headquarters to the far end of that winter range, which was around fifteen miles, returning to the ranch at night.

My main top saddle horse was a short-backed sturdy little grey horse that I broke myself, and called Smokey. Smokey was a real lovable saddle horse, with a whole pile more sense than a lot of people I know of — you could talk to him and, ears forward, he seemed to take in every word you said. His shining dark eyes looked at me, as if to say, "You're my friend, old-timer." And I sure, sure was.

Smokey got to be a real cow-horse and I was sure proud of the way he could cut a cow and calf out of a bunch, or a beef steer. With no effort at all he turned this way and that, and very seldom ever made a miscue. It would have been a real hard decision to make, as to which was the best cow-horse, Smokey or old Sunny Jim, as both were real toppers. However, by this time, old Sunny was finished. All good cow-horses wear out if you keep on ariding them along for any length of time. Only once did I ever give old Smokey to anyone else to ride. On that occasion, unbeknown to me, this fellow rode him so hard, and then let him stand in the barn covered with frost and sweat on his hair that Smokey caught pneumonia. I had a hell of a touch-and-go time to get old Smokey better. From then on I was the only one to ride Smokey.

We shipped our beef cattle by live weight again that fall and Mr. Bob Cromie put in his beef drive with ours and we shipped them out at the 59 Mile stockyards, in the same style and programme that we had done in former years.

At this time a very ticklish, and loaded with hard feelings, situation came about in our range country between the cattlemen and the horse owners on the range. Much of the ill feeling was produced by the fact that cowmen had, of necessity, to bring their cattle in off the range in the late fall, to feed and winter them, and the horse owner boys used to let their animals run on the range all the year around. The result was that when the grass just started to grow, which it did as soon as the snow went away and the warm sun started to warm up the earth, on the open hills and flats, the horses, and there sure were lots of them, used to eat that young grass right down as fast as it came up so that when the cows were turned out on the range there was very little left.

The cattlemen had to have a grazing permit every summer to run their cattle on the government range and the horse owners were supposed to have a permit also, but very few of them bothered to apply for one. While the horses did no harm to the range in the late fall and winter months, there is no doubt that for the first six weeks of the growing season, the horses sure raised hell with the young grass.

Anyone, at this time, could be a horse rancher without too much trouble or expense, as all he needed was a stud and some cayuse mares, a branding iron and a brand, a good lasso rope and a couple of good saddle horses, some sort of a corral and a camping place, and he was all set for business.

There was certainly a lot of ill-feeling in this Clinton, Big Bar country amongst the ranchers, the cow men claiming they had to pay grazing fees and the horse men paid nothing and got twelve months use of the grass. The government was fully aware of this, but, as usual, any government has its ears to the ground, and must never do anything that would hurt the Grand Old Party. With politics and votes in mind, for a long time, they refused to do anything. The government knew they could not do much with the horses if they seized them for grazing payments whereas if a cattleman did not pay his grazing fees, the department jumped on him, like a duck on a June bug, and took him to court where he got fines or some confiscation.

In the final jumps, the government said they could not afford the expense of rounding up these horses, a whole pile of which were unbroken and never used so they hired horse-shooters to shoot these horses down in the late fall and winter months. The shooters were given five dollars per head, a condition being that the shooter must produce the scalp and ears of each horse.

I was fairly active in our local stock association in these years and while I was certainly in favour of cutting down these big bands of range horses, sometimes as many as twenty in a bunch, I also was very strongly in favour of a proposal to round up all these horses and shoot down any that could not be run into a corral, then sell them for fox meat and dog food. A pair of horsehide gloves cost around $3.00 a pair, and there were sure a lot of pairs of gloves in a horsehide, tanned and smoothed out.

I knew if the boys got a few dollars out of their horses, it wouldn't be too rough for them, but for a man to ride up and see his horses laying dead and scalped was a sight that would make him feel mad and mean, and ready to study retaliation. Ranchers being more or less kind of vulnerable, I didn't think the shooting was a good idea. However, the Department refused to listen to any rounding up and sale ideas, so over four hundred horses were shot in that one winter. There were certainly thirty to forty horses that I had turned outside on the range which belonged to the O K Ranching Company.

The matter of trying to find any other buyers outside of fox and dog meat buyers, was almost impossible, as the farm tractors had begun to displace work horses.

The horse population in this area had been cut down to what they once were, and a lot of horse owners ship their old and unwanted horses for fox meat and dog meat, getting a fair price for them. Today, while there is no sale for work horses, a good saddle horse will always be needed. The whole horse question has been better regulated since the years of their great abundance.

I must relate an incident that happened down in that Spences Bridge range country, around this time.

There was quite a lot of hard feelings between the cow men and the Indian horse owners and things came to such a high tension that a meeting was called at a well-located school house. The ranchers showed up in good cars and old half-wore-out jalopies. The Indians came by saddle horses and teams and buggies.

The local Forest Ranger took charge of the meeting and addressed all the folks gathered there, telling them that something had to be done about this horse question. The horses were eating around eighty acres of grass each as against the range cattle eating around forty acres to the head in the six months' grazing season. The cattlemen were really aboiling because they had range fees to pay while the horse owners paid nothing. The ranger suggested that the benevolent government in Victoria would pay the Indians, and other horse owners, five dollars a head for each horse shot, or for each horse delivered to them.

This offer kind of looked good to the young Indians but the old Indians received it in stony silence except every now and then when some of them would let out a loud gutteral sound in their own language. It sounded like "umpah" and their grizzled, lined old faces registered what they thought of the ranger's proposition.

A young and ardent preacher who had only been in the range country for a few months, was there and figured that he would enlarge his circle of followers. The whole gathering of whites and

Indians rough-locked in their talks and the young preacher, with an ever-consuming ideal of doing good, asked if he could speak a few words to the ranchers and Indians. The ranger told him to go ahead if he thought he could do anything to help. Well, sir, the young preacher went all out, and exhorted the folks to come to some sort of agreement. He told the Indians in real eloquent words that the Great White Father in Victoria would never be low enough to do "God's Children of the Ranges" any harm and he begged them to work together with the ranchers in the matter of cleaning up the horses. The old Indian boys just looked sternly ahead and said nothing, except every once in a while one of them would let go with a throaty, gutteral blast of "umpah."

The meeting broke up and the ranger and the preacher were the last to leave the school house. The preacher boy was feeling quite pepped up as he figured he had made a direct hit with the Indian bucks and the ranchers. He said he was impressed and intrigued by that soft sounding word, "umpah," that the old Indians had used so frequently.

The ranger meditated a minute or so, cut himself off a fair-sized chew off his plug of chewing tobacco and looked right square at the preacher. "Do you know anything of the Indian language?" he asked. The young fellow replied, "Oh no, but I shall be immensely delighted to learn." The ranger said gently, "Well, this word 'umpah' in the Indian language means bullshit — nothing more or less." The young preacher boy headed for home, and I guess he learned something that day.

I've often had time to do some thinking and studying as I went along the old trail, and I believe that the old Indian word "umpah" has had a farther reaching effect on the world's history than many things, and I'm sure that old "umpah" has won a lot more battles than a whole army of machine-gunners.

We wintered a lot of our cattle down on the Crow's Bar winter range again in 1944. I had Jim Fletcher, an old prospector, keeping the shoreline broken up and clear in a couple of places along the river. It was a small job, but it has to be done every day without fail for about ten weeks, the reason being that if the cattle went out on the shore-ice — which sometimes ran out twenty to thirty feet — they might slip or slide off the ice into the river and get a free ride down to Vancouver, only they'd be drowned a long time before they got there. The situation needed watching, so old Jim broke the ice away, clear back up to the river bank every morning. I always kept a couple of blocks of salt near the two water holes, about a mile or more apart. The cattle got used to coming to the salt at the good safe watering hole. I know this little game saved a dozen head of cattle every winter.

Jim Fletcher was sure a great hand to talk to himself. He would be talking and shouting out loud in his cabin and at different times when I'd be sitting on old Smokey, he'd be really laying down the law to someone, but as soon as I'd knock on his door he'd come to the door and talk quite naturally to me. I never joshed the old fellow about it, as I know lots of folks who kind of half talk to themselves, especially when they live alone. One of these old boys once told me, "Talking to yourself is not too bad, Harry, but if you get to answering yourself, you are really heading for trouble." A man who has lived alone for a long time don't get along any too well living or working with other people.

I knew an old fellow, Charlie Jones, who lived all alone below Meadow Lake years ago, the road arunning right past his door a few yards. I came along there on real cold day, a miserable raw wind kind of sneaking over the ice on the lake. It was late and crawling on towards night too and I was a long ways from any place that I could camp so I climbed down off my horse and knocked on his door. He opened the door a few inches and I asked if I could stay overnight and feed my horse a bite of hay in his barn. Old Charlie was over sixty years old, I guess, and he had been there quite awhile alone and seldom ever went anywhere. I had heard that he had been an old cowhand in the Dakota-Montana country and had got into a jack-pot back there and shot a fellow dead. I've an idea that he was kind of expecting to see some of this fellow's friends come ahunting him up. I only saw him outside in Clinton once, and when he came into the hotel room he glanced all around and went and sat down in a chair right in the angle of the two walls. No doubt he wasn't going to let anyone get behind him.

He always slept with his .45 right under his pillow, so I was kind of sure myself that he'd been in a jack-pot of some kind. Charlie had two cabins side by side, sleeping in one and cooking in the other. After I'd tended my horse, I walked over and went in and being cold I stood close to the cook-stove. Charlie was mixing up a pan of biscuits for supper. I hadn't been there more than a minute before he barked, "Harry, I'm going to make you a fire in the other cabin and you can sit there. I'll call you when I'm ready for yer to eat." I said, "Why, Charlie, don't go to all that trouble, I can set here all right." So Charlie said, "God Almighty! I just can't cook nor nothin' if someone is in the same room." He walked out and made a fire in the other cabin and I went and sat there till he called me. All supper time we never spoke a word, and after supper I got up and went in the other cabin and set there till it came time to get under some old blankets and go to sleep.

Charlie told me once, and once is all he had to tell me, "You know, I just don't want nobody to talk to me, Harry. If anyone talks to me it just gets me right off my chain of thoughts, and I don't like it worth a damn."

I only saw old Charlie about once or twice after that, and just said "Howdy" to the old fellow, that's all. I heard that after he left the Meadow Lake country, he went to old Mexico and I've been told that Mexicans are very happy people, so I don't know how he made out down there.

Chapter 18

The Honourable Jack Goes Over the Mountain

THE RANCH OPERATION IN 1944 was on a much reduced and labour-saving style, as it was a very hard matter to get any kind of help, except real elderly men, so I ran the O K with a skeleton crew, worked long hours myself, and got along the best I could. The rest of the ranching element had to do much the same thing.

Every ounce of available labour and natural resources were used by our country. The boys made a landing in France that summer, and there were many of our folks giving all their time and energy in helping out with Red Cross work, trying to raise war loan funds, blood donations and working in munitions. I'd say the number of slackers was almost negligible. When I'd get to studying on the great war efforts of our old Canada, I kind of always got a feeling of being proud and sort of privileged, to know I was a Canadian.

Some bad news came along for me that summer by the fact that one of our boys who had left the ranch to go overseas, Jimmie Grinder, was killed in action. He was sure a good lad, and his old dad, Johnnie, took it pretty hard for quite awhile.

Later on, when I was up at the lake putting up hay, I got another jolt hearing that our Bill MacDonald was posted as missing and brought down out of the air on the Roumanian front. I called to mind Bill telling me he didn't want to go, but just figured he'd ought to. War is a rough game and death and casualties have got to be expected and encountered, but I felt pretty bitter and mean about it just the same, as I remembered only too well the days of World War I in which I had done my share.

Mr. Harrison was up at the ranch staying at the main O K and he picked up a severe jolt of pneumonia. I was up haying at the lake when this happened and at once I jumped on old Smokey and never quit trotting or loping along till I reached the O K where I found my old partner just astaggering up and down, kind of half knocked out, and not even knowing whether he was afoot or on horseback, with a high temperature. However, his capable son-in-law, Dr. Ward Turvey, arrived and brought along a special nurse from Vancouver. After a few days Mr. Harrison started to rally, and when he arrived at the stage when he was starting to pick up again, his competent wife came to the ranch, and personally looked after him till he got all right again.

George was always a real hardy type of man, and not subject to much sickness of any kind and up to this time he never failed to show he could surely take it and like it, same as the rest of us boys. I remember one year at the O K when there were two young fellows who never got up till the breakfast was sitting right under their noses on the table. Mr. Harrison and I both figured these boys were just getting plain lazy, and he said, "Harry, I'm going to show these boys a real good way to freshen themselves up in the morning, and start the day off right." Next morning I had just come back from the barn where I'd been feeding and watering the horses, and I came in the house and heard Mr. Harrison holler to the boys, "Follow me, fellows. I'll show you how to wake up in the morning. Come out of that bed and follow me." Down the stairs he came, not a stitch of clothes on, right in his birthday suit, and walked out of the front porch and rolled around in that five inches of snow, and came back in the house again. The two young bucks had got out of bed by this time and were standing on the floor looking at him, kind of half-shivering in their underwear. I at once sized up the situation, and without a word, started to shed my britches and get down to my birthday suit too. George said, "Where are you going, Harry?" I said, "Mr. Harrison, nobody sixty-eight years old is going to show *me* up the hard way. I'm going out there too." George looked at me and said, "Damned if I don't like it so well that I'll come out with you!" So both of us went out and rolled around in the snow several times, and came back in the house. I told the boys to try it, it felt fine, and while a lot of fellows could brag about the hair on their chest, it took quite a man to roll around with snow on his chest, but, of course, the young fellows thought we were crazy.

I was always an early riser. I mind the time when I first came out to our Canada. I started out with a rugged Canadian Irishman for eight dollars a month and my board and he worked hell out of me, and himself too. His early morning cry at quarter to five in the morning was, "Ain't you afraid the sun will burn a hole in your backside?" I'd be out before you could say scat.

The winter of 1944 faded out, another year came sliding in and there were little or no changes in our ranch operation. We confined our efforts to raising hay and selling our grass-fed beef cattle at on-the-hoof prices. We reduced our hog efforts down to six brood sows and their litters, with not too much profit on them as our grain was all bought and shipped in from the outside. Sometimes when we'd be talking about hogs and the expenses of feeding them, Mr. Harrison would look at me, smile and say, "Well, the water the hogs drink is still free, Harry." However, I had no choreman around then, and all the hog feeding and cow milking was done by myself almost all the time. Once in awhile I'd get Uncle Bill or Ronnie to spell me off, if I had to be away. Our slaughterhouse was a forgotten issue these years — except once in a while I'd kill a small critter for the ranch or Big Bar Lake where Peg was still going strong in the guest and fishing business.

I received the good news that Bill MacDonald had been heard from, and not missing as reported. While Bill was wounded seriously, he had escaped into Russian hands. The Russians had looked after him and in time he was returned to England for further medical treatment.

The last part of May and early June of that year saw the collapse of the entire German armies in Europe. It had taken a lot of concentrated energies to upset these fanatical aggressors. The great military power and well-organized industrial speed-up of the United States without doubt turned the scales in our favour and later in the summer the Japanese armies and navy in the Pacific folded up, as the Japs could not stand or resist, the terrible impact of the two atomic bombs dropped on their country.

I had quite a character of a man working on the ranch that year. His name was Slim Barrow, and he was a tall fellow with a very jaded face, a serious, high-strung sort of man. But you can never tell by looking at a frog how far he can jump and Slim was a real handyman at most all kinds of ranch work, particularly around the blacksmith shop. Slim had one terrible fault. He just simply could not be depended on if there was any liquor around, so I done my best to try and stop him from getting any, as he didn't have brains enough to last him overnight when it came to handling liquor.

After Slim had been there about six weeks or so he came to me and asked if I could write him a cheque for one hundred dollars. I hunted up his sheet in my ranch wages book and found that he only had sixty-five dollars coming, so I said, "Slim, you've only got sixty-five bucks coming so I can't give you the hundred you want." Slim was very disappointed-looking, and asked me if I would lend him the extra thirty-five dollars, as he wanted to buy a second-hand car in Clinton for the hundred dollars. Slim promised me by all and holy that he'd come right back from Clinton next day with the car, and would work the other thirty-five bucks out on the ranch. I always tried to be something of a human being — and sometimes got a damned good skinning for being that way — so I listened to his urgent pleading for the extra thirty-five bucks. Slim goes out on the stage to Clinton, telling me that he'll be back next day for sure, him and the old car. Well, sir, next day comes along and the day after, and no signs of Slim. A week later out comes Slim on the stage from Clinton. He looks at me kind of sideways and ashamed-looking, and I'm ready to fire him, but he's got that thirty-five bucks "in" to the O K Ranching Company and I'm not going to let him go till that's worked out. After awhile I got the whole story when I got a letter from the Ashcroft Hotel telling me that one of my employees, a certain Slim, had got on a big drunk around the hotel, and had filled not only one bed, but two beds, and there was a laundry bill for thirty-six dollars, so please would I write out a cheque at once and send them the thirty-six dollars. I told Slim he was a hell of a man to trust, and never again. Slim, of course, like any other drunk, had a raft of excuses. However, I kept him long enough to get my thirty-five back, and the laundry bill to the hotel paid, and then I let him go, not without giving him an offer to quit booze entirely, which he refused to do, so he and I both wrote finis to our connection, and he lost a good home.

Sometime later I was in Ashcroft, and when I walked into the hotel the owner, Mr. Johnson, seeing me got up out of his old chair and growled at me like an old she-bear, telling me what a hell of a ranch I must be running up there at the O K to have such low-down coyotes as Slim on my payroll. I listened to Mr. Johnston till he was all finished and over with his "mad on" and then I said with a smile, "Mr. Johnson, don't take it so hard, because whenever one of the Big Bar pilgrims comes along and gets so full he just can't feel his backside if he took both hands, and leaves his card in your bed, it's a sure sign he loves you and wants to be good tillicums." I must say that Mr. Johnson gave me a real hard look, not knowing whether I was crazy, or just plain ornery.

Booze has sure been the downfall of this Cariboo Country in many ways, as there is no happy medium about most of our boys. Rum drinking, playing the fiddle and not paying the bills, has put many a family out of ranch and home in this country up and down both sides of the Fraser River. The government baiting the boys along, selling them booze, and the Mounties throwing them into the jug for a spell, or fining them if they get too much, and the beer-parlour boys who need no one to advertize their business, as their customers walk in like trained pigs to hand them their hard-earned bucks.

The common sense game of having a drink before supper after a busy day is a real worthwhile and time-honoured custom, but then put the bottle away in the cupboard. The trouble is that most people never stop till they see the bottom of the bottle.

In May of 1945 I was deputized as one of a committee of cattlemen to go down to Vancouver and attend a meeting in which the Premier of British Columbia, the Honourable John Hart, who was a fine old gentleman, and the directors of the P.G.E. were all there.

We had the object in mind to convince the Premier and the directors that our province should undertake to complete the P.G.E. from Squamish to Vancouver to eliminate having to have our cattle transported by barge and tug-boat into that metropolis. The conditions the rancher had to contend with were very detrimental. Seasickness and awaiting favourable tides, presented unfortunate results for the beef shipper and the meat packer alike.

The Premier agreed to give the matter his earnest consideration, but nothing was done till quite a few years later. I really think that from that meeting and the relentless pressure put on the government by the folks from our Cariboo did, in after years, accomplish the job of finishing this railroad.

Sometimes in the old game of life, the sunshine breaks through the fog and cloud of everyday existence when you leastways expect it. At this time the Cariboo, Okanagan, and Nicola Valley cattlemen started to work on the idea of co-operative effort, which I had been talking and pleading for amongst the cattlemen for years, and they formed a co-operative association, the idea being that the beef cattle of our interior would be sold through a selling agency *belonging to the ranchers*, and the elimination of the personal sale to the packer.

For quite a little while the response of some of the cattlemen, especially the larger operators, was luke warm, but as time progressed more and more of the boys sold their cattle through this agency. The widespread difference in prices the producer is paid, in comparison to the prices the consumer has to pay, is always a bitter reflection in the mind of the ranchers. I remember receiving four cents a pound for good steers by live weight, and the following day in a big department store in Vancouver, I paid twenty-two cents a pound for a humble pot roast, or chuck roast as it is called, which is just one jump ahead of boiling beef and stew bones.

Our cattle were priced by a qualified cow-man, hired by the association, who sold them to the meat packers and I'm sure this method gives us better prices, especially in the case of the small ranchers, of which the association is largely composed. The large operator always seemed to get a little better deal in selling his beef to the packers — at least a lot of us thought along those lines.

The British Columbia Livestock Co-Operative Association now disposes of at least eighty-five per cent of all the cattle sold in the interior. While it is not a cure-all for all the problems of the cattlemen, it is the best and first step in the right direction. It is my final hope and prayer that the time may come when the rancher's calf, from the time it is born out on the bunch-grass sidehills to the day when the beef-critter is wrapped up and passed over a counter, will put some of the financial gravy into the rancher's hands.

The last stages of World War II having just about come to an end, our boys returned home to our Canada. I rejoiced to see our Bill MacDonald and Joe Murdoch, and a lot of the boys return. I found that they were now much more ambitious in their aims and ideas of progress for themselves. I could see that they were not at all interested in staying with me on the O K Ranch and I wished them the best of luck.

Bill got married to a very nice girl, named Beth Handy, who was living in Clinton and they settled down in the town. Bill became a partner in a garage and a butcher shop business in Clinton. Joe Murdoch became a machine-operator in a big copper mine which I believe is in the lower Nicola country. These boys were far more mature in their thinking after their return from overseas.

Most of our cattle wintered down on the Crow's Bar winter range except for some thin cows and the calves and the bulls. I rode down every week or sometimes Ronnie did. He was now taking a man's place around the O K and was real good on a horse around cows, and a good man around machinery or tractors and trucks, which helped quite a lot, as I had put in my active years mostly around horses and was not very well used to the gas and oil age that was sweeping over the farm and ranch areas all through the west.

We had a pretty fair hay crop that summer of 1946 and I was busy doing all I could to save high wages and cope with the shortage of help. I had five of us that year in the haying. Myself, Ronnie, Uncle Bill and two other old fellows. One of them done the cooking for the rest of us and sometimes I was lucky enough to get an old Indian pal of mine to help for a little while. The summer was well advanced when one evening just after I had gone to bed, I heard the telephone ring. I jumped out of bed to answer it and it was a long-distance call from Vancouver from a young Brigadier Bill Roaf who was the son of "The Honourable" Jack Roaf. This young man had had a remarkable progress record while serving overseas and had attained the high rank of Brigadier General. He informed me that his dad had passed on over the Big High Mountain and I at once headed for Vancouver to help carry out my old friend and O.C. of World War I days.

Many years earlier, "The Honourable" Jack Roaf had led us into the large Anglican Christ Church Cathedral for Divine Service in army days. Little did I expect that the second time I was to be in that quiet and majestic emblem of the Christian faith I would be helping to carry my old friend out to the graveyard.

I always hated to have to go to any funeral, it seems so final somehow, and yet I believe that death is just a matter of changing your "range" and a human being's tour through this old "valley of tears" is just a drop in the bucket of ageless time. I've often done a little studying on these things, and wondered on the problem. Sizing it all up, I came to the conclusion that when a fellow is a baby he gets a three-foot crib to lie down in, and after seventy years or more of going like hell with feverish haste, and worrying because he can't get more money, or power, or both, and after all this fuss, fun, frolic and a lot of bitchery, all he gets out of it is a six-foot "crib." What a run and rat-race for seventy years, just to gain three feet in the end!

Such is life! Maybe it's a good thing that we can't tell definitely what lies ahead of us. It's one great secret that the good Lord ain't going to let us in on.

I sure did regret the passing of "The Honourable John" and missed his sound judgment and common sense philosophy which was always a strong source of inspiration to me. I'm proud to know that I still have a strong bond of friendship with his family, in particular Brigadier Bill Roaf, who lives in the same traditions that endeared his honourable dad to me.

Fall and winter came along, and all in all we got by in good shape with very little loss in our cattle. The winter range at Crow's Bar was always a great hay-saver for us, which also meant a big saving in our overhead expenses. The year 1947 brought along some changes in our routine, and changes took place in ways of shipping beef cattle.

Chapter 19

Parting with the OK

We started to ship our cattle by truck to Ashcroft, and on the Canadian Pacific Railway. We put up a solid corral and loading chute and the cattle trucks came right up to the ranch, loaded up, and headed for Ashcroft, seventy-one miles away. This method provided a lot faster shipping service to Vancouver and less shrinkage than by shipping on the P.G.E. which at that time had not been completed. It took only about four hours and a half to truck a load of cattle to Ashcroft, and another eight hours to land them in Vancouver, so that the cattle more or less arrived in the big city all in one day's trip.

This method did away with most of the old beef drives to the shipping point, and with the exception of perhaps one or two large operators, the policy of trucking the cattle shipment has been in fashion ever since.

I found that as long as a cattle truck is moving, and is loaded plumb full, the cattle rode along pretty good. It is the stopping for any length of time that makes the cattle restless and inclined to jump around. I also learned that it was better for the cattle, and there was less shrinkage in travelling, if they got no water for several hours before loading. They stood the trip better.

The old order of things changes with the times and the old time-honoured beef and cattle drives are now a thing of the past, as regards shipping cattle. The gas and oil contraptions take the place of the old cow-hands in this deal. I could not help but have regret at the passing of the old beef drives. There was always a sense of responsibility and good judgment in handling a bunch of beef, or even range cattle, on a drive. The travel was slow, never more than around two miles an hour, with a rest-up for a few minutes every so often, and a fairly long break around noon. The strongest and best cattle were always in the lead, and the lesser ones always in the tail-end of the herd. Sometimes the leaders had to be slowed down so that the weaker ones could travel and stand the pace better. There was always a morning count-up of the bunch, and a check-up at the end of the day's drive, the fellow in charge doing the count as the cattle would string by him in twos and threes.

The cutting-out of the steers, heifers, and dry cows all called for a fellow who knew cattle, and knew how to handle a good cow-horse in a herd. The personal interest a fellow had in certain ones in the herd, maybe the line-backed roan steer or the brockle-faced old-timer of a fat cow, all these things were part and parcel of being an up-to-snuff observing cowboy.

There were just two things that perhaps made the trucking of cattle a better deal than beef drives. One was that cattle driven a long ways tend to become sore-footed on the trails and leg weary, and limping-along beef soon lose weight. The other is the element of time. Nowadays there is a shortage of good reliable help on a drive — the fast disappearing old-time cowboy who took everything in his stride, good and bad, like my old friend, Shell McClane, who used to sleep with his head on a rock so he wouldn't be sleeping too long at any time, and he'd wake up easy.

I'm told that the boys down in Uncle Sam's country have been trucking their cattle for a long time now, so I've always noticed that whatever happens in the States generally comes to us in the matter of perhaps a few months or years, and whether we like it or not it seems like to me that the fortunes of the States and of our Canada are real closely interwoven and almost parallel to each other.

I had an interesting experience in the summer of 1947 when I was nominated by the Clinton Cattlemen's Association to go to Kamloops where there was an Enquiry Commission of six men, sent up from Victoria by the government, to investigate unfair conditions of collecting nearly all the school taxes from the ranchers and farmers.

When I arrived at the court-house in Kamloops I found several of the real big operators of our interior. The Douglas Lake, Gang Ranch, Guichon's of Nicola, Kosters of Canoe Creek and Empire Valley were all there and ready to state their case and their protests. Each of us told our story to the commission and urged them to consider the unequal method of school tax collection. The ranches paid school taxes on thousands of acres, in many instances miles away from any school, and with little or no benefit, whereas, the fellow by the side of the road, with perhaps several children going to school, and owning little, if any, property was paying a very small percentage school tax and getting all the benefits of education for his kids.

I have never heard of a rancher who was opposed in any way to the value of education, but the method of collecting these school taxes is a distinctly unfair deal to the ranchers as a whole. The Government Commission listened to the boys without comment, taking in what was said, and giving us the usual government syrup about doing their best to look into the matter. However, nothing has ever been done towards any change. The ranchers always have been a politically weak bunch of folks, incapable of making a real effective noise with the government powers that be and it looks to me that the present situation will stand indefinitely.

In this same year there was an agreement reached between Mr. Harrison, Peg and myself, in which Peg could purchase the lake property from the O K Ranching Company. Peg had never had much interest in ranching of any kind, and for years had worked long hours in the summer months at Big Bar Lake Guest Ranch. Being a strong individualistic type, she felt that she should be allowed to purchase the lake property. So, after some discussion on the question, Mr. Harrison and I agreed that Peg could buy the property, which she did in that year and realized her long ambition to own her own business. Since that time she has owned and directed the affairs of the lake property without any help or support from myself, making a comfortable living for herself by close attention to the wishes and well-being of her guests and fishermen each summer.

We had a long spell of wet weather in our haying season of that year, and the O K continued along with a very small crew of myself, Ronnie, Uncle Bill and an elderly fellow called Ray Larson. Uncle Bill, or "The Colonel" as some of the boys used to call him, in spite of his seventy years odd, was still right up on the bit and doing an active part in the day-by-day ranch operation.

I was very amused once, when a Vancouver gentleman who was staying at the ranch for a few days, took me to one side and asked me if it was really true that Uncle Bill had been a colonel in the Canadian Armed Forces. I told the gentleman that I was kind of sure that Uncle Bill had never reached the rank of colonel, but all of us on Big Bar Creek felt that a prominent area like the Creek and the Howling Dog Dance Hall, should be entitled to at least one honorary colonel. Away down in the deep southeastern States, we were told, pretty nigh every second negro had the title of "Jedge," so our title of "The Colonel" to old Uncle Bill was a real honour to the ranch and our South Cariboo country.

We shipped our beef and some veal calves that fall, taking them from the ranch to the Canadian Pacific railroad at Ashcroft. We took the best possible care to see that the cattle reached Ashcroft and were weighed just as soon as possible. The shrinkage in weight in a calf is quite high, as just as quick as your calf finds out he can't get to his ma for a friendly nuzzle or a little warm milk, he begins to fret and worry and that certainly makes a difference in his weight in a few hours. From the meat packer's end of it, the quicker the veal calf has his final exit, the better for the packer's pocket-book, so we really done our best to avoid delays and hold-ups in transit, and the packer rushed them to the coast by the first available stock-car.

Christmas Day was always a happy day at the O K. Peg had a Christmas tree with lots of decorations and presents on it and we had a good turkey with all the trimmings. There was me with my good suit of clothes on and a necktie, which was just like a stranger round my neck. Good cigars, and a couple good snorts of O.B. Joyfull to round out the festive day, and I'd have a real bellyful of good grub, and I'd be happy with my thoughts, and our little family and the boys working there. Our Edwin always had his Christmas with us at the O K and I made it my rule to put aside, for that day anyway, any rough problems or routine bitchery and concentrate on having one day's peace with the world.

Well, sir, just as sure as Hell is a mantrap, two days after Christmas there came a ten-inch fall of snow. As soon as that cleared off, the old mountains back of the ranch took on their grey, cold and frosty look, and we were into thirty-five below zero almost overnight, and everything at the O K was eating hay, with the exception of the cattle we had on the winter range at Crow's Bar.

I had a lot of real dirty days riding that winter. The snow was deep over the mountains and I'd make pretty slow time riding along till I got on the brow of the hill, going down on to the winter range along the river. The return ride with the sun gone down, and the darkness and cold settling in was a real cold mean trip. I couldn't hurry old Smokey along when he had around two feet of snow to buck for several long miles. I'd get home with the frost hanging on to my face and nose and eyelashes. Smokey's old face and hair were just covered with frost too, but a fairly warm barn, some good hay and a feed of oats, a rub down with a wisp of dry hay and wiping the frost off him, straightened him out. That fine, almost human horse, would turn his head in his stall and look at me as if to say, "Thanks old-timer." I'd head for the house where I'd get a hot drink and a big feed of mulligan, then I'd almost always get drowsy after being out in the cold air all day and I'd fall asleep in a chair or on a sofa, waking up some hours later and getting into bed.

This weather condition kept up for a long time that winter, with snow and still more snow falling, and real low forty below zero temperatures after each fall of snow. It stayed with us until the last week of April of 1948, and we woke up in the last few days in April with only three loads of hay left, which was a very serious situation for us to be in, as the snow was still deep and crusted on the higher levels, and no sign of any feed in sight.

I figured we just had to get our cows to some feed somehow.

While we had some cattle on the winter range at Crow's Bar, we had been feeding quite a few at the O K and how to get the O K cows over to the windswept sidehills just above the winter range, where some grass was sticking up out of the snow, confronted me with quite a problem.

Anyhow, Ronnie and I, Uncle Bill and a real all-round cowhand named Harry Grinder, a son of my old friend, Billy, all broke trail by riding on horses, one behind the other, through that crusted deep snow on Big Bar Mountain. Then we strung our cows out one behind the other, and after a very long hard trip we got them over to the half-bare sidehills above the winter range, where they could get a bite to eat on that bunch-grass. It was sure a nip and tuck set-up, but we made it, and we sure had horse-shoes around our necks and the good Lord ariding right along with us, or we'd have lost quite a few of our cows that were real heavy in calf before the final break-up came in early May.

I guess in this old world, it is quite fair and true to figure that troubles never come along in single file — there's always an odd one or two extra. After coming through a real tough winter, word came to me that the fine old Gang Ranch had sold out all their holdings to two American go-getters named Bill Studdert of Seattle, and Floy Skelton of Idaho Falls in the U.S.A.

This meant to us that the famous Crow's Bar pasture which the O K Ranching Company was renting from the Gang Ranch, had to be turned over to the new owners, who wanted to keep it for themselves and their operation.

I felt the loss of the Crow's Bar pasture very keenly, as I had spent several years there in my early days, and had been renting it from the Gang for seven years, and I knew it was a real money-maker and money-saver for any cattleman, running and wintering cattle. So the O K lost a very valuable unit to them. As the layout involved a lot of money, Mr. Harrison and I felt that we could not afford to buy it.

We plugged along that summer putting up every forkful of hay we could find, and put in a stack, knowing that from now on our cattle would have to depend on hay-feeding all winter. Now that the Crow's Bar winter range had gone it became necessary to try and build up our hay fields to the best all-out production.

Over a matter of a few months, I had been wondering as to the problem of Mr. Harrison's interest in the O K Ranching Company, and while I knew that his son, George, and the two daughters, Mrs. Turvey and Nora, were all on a most friendly relationship to myself, I was also certain that they had no active desire to own or operate the O K Ranch. Beyond a few days change and a holiday, the ranch held no important consideration to them. Of course, Mr. Harrison always loved the "big outdoors" and had an untiring interest in all the day by day and seasonal activities of the ranch, this no doubt being a reflex of his early life in Manitoba. I suggested that if he liked I would try and buy out his share in the O K Ranching Company and after a lot of serious deliberation Mr. Harrison sold me his interest in the old ranch, reserving the big house he had built in earlier years for his own use.

This situation, of course, made not the slightest difference in the friendship, love and respect I had for this old fine gentleman, his wife and the family. Nothing on earth could ever change me in that great association that we had had for so many years. If it had not been for his help and wise counsel, and generous dealings with the O K Ranch, all those years, the ranch welfare and progress would have been seriously retarded.

I carried along with Uncle Bill and Ronnie, just trying to get a little help whenever I could, mainly in the haying season, which was our busiest time. I redoubled my efforts to get along with as little overhead expense as possible.

In the late winter of 1948, Ronnie just narrowly escaped a pretty rough finish when his brown saddle horse, with sharp shoes on at that, slid down a steep bank for quite a few yards. Ronnie managed to grab hold of a strong little fir limb and threw his feet out of the stirrups, but the horse kept on asliding towards the creek. Ronnie pulled himself together, and bit by bit got around the steep bank and up on to a trail where he walked home getting back in the pitch dark.

Edwin was down at the ranch from the lake for a few days and next morning he and Ronnie rode up to where the jack-pot had taken place. Edwin took a turn around a small tree with a long rope and let Ronnie down the steep bank to where he could see his saddle lying on the ground. The saddle cinch must have busted, as somehow old Shorty, the horse Ronnie was riding, had kicked or rolled the saddle off. Anyway, Ronnie got his saddle back and a little while later saw Shorty standing in the creek bottom with some other horses. Later Ronnie rode a different trail into the creek and caught up his horse.

Ice on the trails and sidehills, particularly those sidehills facing the north are really bad medicine in the winter months. Even if a horse is pretty well shod with sharp shoes and never-slip caulks in them, things sometimes happen awful quick with little or no warning.

In the spring of 1949, I tried out one more round of trying to put in a two hundred acre crop of wheat on Big Bar Mountain, but the old mountain ran true to form again in real dry farm style and after all the work and effort there was only two hundred dollars gravy for our trouble, after all the wages, gas and oil bills and overhead were paid. That was the absolute final closing up of any dry farm operation. It was just no good.

We had pretty fair hay crops in the summer of 1949. Our Uncle Bill did most of the irrigating the hay fields, while Ronnie and I looked after the ranch fences and the cattle, except when the haying season came along.

Uncle Bill was a real top-hand irrigator and used to live in a cabin about three miles from the main ranch buildings. He did all his own cooking and Bill's cabin was always as clean as a new pin. Every Sunday was his bath and washing day and he would never miss that weekly washing under any kind of circumstances. I know I would have had a hard time to replace him, although sometimes he and I would have quite a bit of arguing back and forth as to the best ways of getting a job done, but we have always been the best of pals. We all loved the old-timer.

That winter Uncle Bill went to the coast and Ronnie and I fed the cattle. We didn't have to start feeding till about the end of January 1950 that winter, which was an easy one.

The aftermath of war and the mix-up in Korea brought a scarcity of good help and the big high wages paid out in industry left a serious situation in regard to any help on a ranch. No one wanted to work, unless they were paid a very high wage, which, of course, the average rancher could not afford. The old loyal type of man, like our Uncle Bill, disappeared from the picture. I was faced with a lot more work and it was more and more difficult to find anyone who had any sense of responsibility towards his job, or the man he was working for.

I had an odd experience on Hallowe'en night, 1949. Needing some money, I had shipped a mixed carload of calves and some dry cows to Ashcroft by truck and had loaded them up in the C.P.R. cattle car late in the evening with Ronnie there to help me. I had been paid for the cattle and Ronnie and I struck out for home in our ranch truck, arriving back at the O K in the early hours of the morning.

About a day or so later, I heard that some of the Hallowe'en boys around Ashcroft had opened the cattle car door and the dry cows had all jumped out of the car and taken to the hills just south of Ashcroft. This proved to be a very poor and expensive joke on the part of those knot-heads as it was quite costly to get the cows rounded up again and sent to the coast. It turned out to be very expensive for the parents of those boys who pulled off such a brainless and know-nothing stunt.

I've often figured that a good, tough, rough army sergeant major or someone with a black snake squirt would be a much more sensible solution for those kind of tricks, rather than hiring the services of some high paid doctor of psychology to tell them, "Oh, please don't be a bad boy."

Democracy is a wonderful set-up and contains many blessings to us, but along with that it is undoubtedly a good cloak for a real son of a b . . . . However, we have only two choices, democracy with its free and easy and often very slack ways of getting good government, or the communistic style of rigid bureaucratic "toe the line or else" form of government. To date no one has ever come up with any other of the happy medium style.

Along about the end of July 1950, there came a tall grey-haired and capable American gentleman to the O K Ranch, and asked me if I would consider selling out. He presented me with quite a problem as I had been living there a long time, with many endless hours of hard work and struggling along to build it up and I found myself very tired, crowding sixty years old and not able to stand the racket half as well as I could in former years.

The ranch had never been a real worthwhile winner, one year with another, most often resulting in keeping the bills fairly well paid up and always having plenty to eat and clothes to wear, and some years a little more than that. On the other hand, I knew that I had lived for a long time in our old Cariboo, which I'm sure is still the best country that ever layed out of doors, and with all its ups and downs, I sure did love the cow business better than anything else I've ever seen, and this is God's Country. I feel sure that He only made one mould of our Cariboo and if He had ever broken the mould He might have decided never to make another and the good Lord had to have a certain number of clodhoppers in His framework of the world and I guess I am one of them.

Accordingly, I sold the O K Ranch to the American business tycoon, a gentleman named Mr. George W. Marshall of Seattle. Like many more of us he has a basic longing for the wide open spaces and a genial smile breaks out on his face as he rides around looking at his fat, sleek cows and calves.

At this time our Cariboo was invaded by a considerable sprinkling of very well-to-do Americans, and they purchased cow outfits and proceeded to modernize them along their own ideas of progress. Today many of our ranches have electric lights, inside plumbing, tractor machinery and even an odd aeroplane shows up sometimes. All of these improvements were practically unknown and entirely out of reach to the earlier generation of my day. There is a lot more money invested in these ranches nowadays. However, these newcomers to our Cariboo have, in most instances, become a very valuable asset to our country. In fact, without the great influx of American money into our Canada, to help build up the resources we have, our progress would have been sadly limited, as no one can run a clothes washing-machine without gas, oil and soap, and no country will ever develop without investing money from some source or other.

Chapter 20

My Last Big Drive

I GUESS THE DAY HAD COME for this old-timer to step aside for progress. In August 1950 I left the O K Ranch after quite a few successes and some failures. The happiest days of my life were when I was going like hell, taking the good and the bad right in my stride, worrying about debts and bills to pay, and often stewing away and worrying about things that could happen, but never did. One thing that always gave me a lot of satisfaction was to reach the end of a day and know I'd done something, most generally worthwhile.

I was sure feeling tired now. I made up my mind I'd do little or nothing for quite awhile, until I'd had a darned good rest anyhow. So I just dogged it for several months, doing just what I'd feel like doing. Late that fall I went down to my old tillicum, Mr. Bob Cromie, and looked after his ranch all winter while he was away at the coast.

In the spring of 1951, I was feeling much better physically, and I came to realize that a man who has had years of active life, just can't sit around and do nothing. It becomes very difficult and unsettling to contend with, and I began to look around. I figured that as I had had quite a long rest, now maybe it would be a good idea to try and do a little something. I had one or two good offers from rancher friends to take over positions of responsibility on their ranches but with the high wages and the problem of finding real good help, I figured maybe I'd have a tough time to get any real results for them, and so I declined with thanks.

In the early part of May of that year, along came Bill Studdert, who was one of the new owners of the Gang Ranch. He wanted me to organize and take a drive of one thousand yearling steers and heifers up to the Gang Ranch from their layout known as the Perry Ranch, which is about four miles south of the Cache Creek crossroads.

I did quite a bit of studying on this as I knew the drive well enough and had been on quite a few drives from the Gang Ranch and Crow's Bar in the earlier days of nearly forty years back. The matter which was giving me a lot of thought was who I could get to help on the drive, who had any experience at all and who was a pretty fair man on a horse and knew something about handling cattle on a trail.

Studdert, in his usual breezy sort of way, promised me he'd get hold of at least six good cowhands to help up on the trip to the Gang. Well, sir, I told him I'd take a chance on bringing them up, so I went up to the Gang Ranch and stayed there for a few days getting in saddle horses, getting them shod for the trip, getting grub, dishes and other things ready, and finally I started for the Perry Ranch, with two cowboys and a cook, the cook being the wife of one of the boys.

It took about two days and a half to drive down there, with a team and a light wagon and when I got there I looked around the yearlings and rounded them up out of the sagebrush flats and on the mountain east of the Perry Ranch, where they were supposed to be in a pasture. After several days riding, I figured that we had them all gathered up and looking them over I noticed quite a lot were in poor shape — looked to me like they had not been fed near enough hay that winter. I don't know whose fault that was, because there were several stacks of alfalfa left over, and when cattle are in poor shape and lots of hay left over it looked like saving a penny and losing a ten-dollar bill to me.

Well, we started out on the drive anyhow, after I had cut out at least seventy-five out of the bunch that I knew for sure would not make the trip, and we plodded along on the same old Cariboo Road of former years. It was changed considerably, as the road was black topped and the string of cars and trucks were travelling back and forth with monotonous regularity.

The little dogies, as we called them, the name generally applied to young steers from the farms and some ranches in the Alberta country, all poked along at around two miles an hour for the first day or so without too much trouble. I got around just as early as I could see to move, figuring that in the first early hours of the morning there would be less cars, trucks and traffic rolling along on the old road and also, it gave the yearlings more time to poke along. Maudie, the cook, who was married to Victor, one of the Indian boys on the drive, was sure a good old gal, and got the campfire going just as soon as daylight peeped up. Her coffee and hot bannocks, and mulligan were just the stuff for hungry cowboys.

We camped outside of Clinton, about a mile, on the third night and I figured that I would string the dogies through the town long before there were any signs of anyone being up. There were an odd one or two Clinton residents, newcomers mostly, who told me it was too bad for me to bring the yearlings through the one and only main street of town because they would make such a mess going through. However, I did not intend to take them a mile or more out of my way, and through different fields and gates just because someone might not like to see or smell cow chips, so I told them, "It's these old chips and the folks that have to live by them are the only things that ever kept this town and country going all these years, and without them, this whole district couldn't have made a living," which was sure a true statement.

Daylight came along and found us all saddled up, and breakfast eaten, and we headed the herd for the town of Clinton just about a mile away. I strung the bunch through Clinton without any trouble of people being up and kids shouting and rattling up the dogies. The only trouble was to keep the town dogs from barking as much as I could, and I finally got the cattle out through the town around half past four in the morning, long before any of the town folks were up, so I guess nobody got their feelings hurt.

We had a lot of bitchery and then some, as we started to climb the long hill out of Clinton, and drifting along towards the old 57 Mile Ranch. The dogies were a lot of them pretty weak and starting to get tired, all the weak ones hanging in the tail-end of the herd and poking along slower than the seven years' itch, but I dare not hurry them, because if I did, or any of the boys did, those dogies would just quit, and once a critter quits and lays down, all the beating on earth won't help a bit.

On top of that we had to pass some sloughs right close to the road and they were full of water, and would mire a bullfrog if it waded out at all in it, for a drink. These dogies coming from that Edmonton area in Alberta, had probebly never seen range water or lakes in their life, more than likely getting their water pumped out of a well into a water trough. When they saw the water in the slough, a lot of them took a drink, and half a dozen got wading out in the water and got bogged down, and I had to rope them and drag them out on my saddle horse.

It was getting well on towards night when we at last got to the 57 Mile, where we were sure glad to camp and gulp down some hot coffee and a big slug of Maudie's mulligan. We rested the dogies all the next day and took it easy and I figured they'd have it easier from there on to the Gang.

I was ham-strung quite a bit on that drive by only having two real good cow-hands with me who knew anything about trailing or handling cattle. The others that Bill Studdert rustled up for me were not worth the powder to blow them to hell, as far as cow-hands went. They needed as much looking after, and more, than the dogies did. One of them in particular, who we nicknamed "Sage Brush Sam," from Cheyenne, Wyoming. He rode along sitting on his horse right in the middle of the herd, and we drove him along with the yearlings. He was useless anyway, so it didn't matter where he was as there was no advantage with that hombre.

After a day's rest, the dogies seemed to have perked up a little and we started out on a sixteen-mile drive to Meadow Lake, and the yearlings travelled along a lot better in that flat and jack-pined timber country, with little or no interruption of any sort, and towards night we got to Meadow Lake and camped again, the dogies getting more feed and grass all the time now, and believe me, these young steers were really throwing the green grass into them, which was sure just what they needed.

The night we arrived at Meadow Lake, along came Bill Studdert and told me to cut out half the herd which we had brought up and take them over to the Crow's Bar pasture for the summer and to leave the other half at Meadow Lake for a few days' rest. Next morning I bunched the whole herd, and cut out just about half of them, and drove them eight miles that day and camped at a little meadow on Big Bar Creek. The following morning I took them over to Crow's Bar pasture, and turned them in to good water and a lot of good grass.

It was sure surprising how quick those dogies responded to lots of grass and good water, and a few cottonwood patches for them to lay down in the shade of. I saw some of these steers two years later and you'd never have recognized them, after being so weak and thin, but that old bunch-grass is better than all the vitamin pills rolled into one. The other half of the drive were taken to the Gang Ranch about two weeks later.

I think that is the last time that I ever heard of any worthwhile drive on the road, and it was my last effort in that line. It would have been a far better success, and away less aggravating, if the cattle had been fat beef cattle, instead of half-fed and thin dogies, with not enough fat on them to grease the hinges of a pair of spectacles.

That job being completed, I'd sometimes ride and help out at the old O K for a few days, and it just seemed to me like going home again. It sure did take me a long time to get used to being away from that old ranch, and a great many times after I left, I'd find myself wishing that I had not sold it, not for any specific reason at all, except that it was home.

About this time a new era broke out on the skyline in our Cariboo country, and timber operators, sawmills and logging concerns all began arriving in the timber areas scattered all through the range country from Ashcroft to Williams Lake, and as far as the Chilcotin. None of us ever considered the great bulk of this fir and jack-pine timber as having any commercial value. However, it turned out that we were entirely wrong in thinking that the only timber worth a damn was located down in the rain belt areas of the coast, or in the northern Prince George country.

Our range country became dotted with small portable mill enterprises and the snarl of a chain saw, and the chug-chug of a logging truck hauling lumber, became everyday commonplace sounds. The fir timber turned into a sea of stumps, tree tops and other down timber which made the matter of riding a saddle horse through these logged-off patches a rough, roundabout and snag-jumping performance. I believe that grazing in these areas has become better, as the sunshine is able to penetrate through the logged-off timber and has made a more favourable class of grass.

With the arrival of sawmills and equipment, there also came a considerable influx of people into our Cariboo. Emigrants arrived from Europe and the war-shaken areas, and a lot of folks from the Prairie Provinces, mainly Saskatchewan and the farm areas there, where the farmers had wakened up and found they couldn't sell the crops they raised. Attracted by high wages, shorter hours and cash money for their work, these folks arrived in big numbers all through our range country. Most of these Prairie boys that I contacted seemed to be real good workers, which I figured was quite natural, as the big majority were from the old farm originally and I've very seldom seen lazy farmers because a lazy farmer just won't survive.

I often think of a visit that a real "political hot-air artist" made to an old friend of mine who lives down in that lower Fraser Valley, not too far from Chilliwack. This fast-talking boy came along at dinner time to my old friend, Jack Morgan, and after having kissed all the babies, and spieling out all his political promises, his mouth going faster than a bell clanger tied to a goose's rear end, he told my friend, Jack, how he'd like to look around such a nice, well-ordered farm. So Jack showed him around his good cowbarns, and the top-hand bunch of good Holstein milk cows and the politician boy was really impressed, telling Jack what a real good setup he had there.

Jack listened to him, and when he'd got through overflowing about what a grand farm he had, my friend turned around to the politician and said, "Mister, you ain't seen the prettiest part about this old farm. Nobody ever talks about it, but it's there just the same." The would-be prime minister was really taken back and said, "For God's sake, let me see this wonderful thing you've not showed me yet." Jack said, "Why, it's the mortgage agin it."

Jack came hunting a time or two on the O K Ranch and he and I both laughed at the story when he told it to me.

The logging industry has grown by leaps and bounds in our range country and I'm kind of sure the gravy from this industry has by far exceeded any gate receipts of the cow business. However, I still think that the game of raising cattle on the range will always be the basic rock and foundation of our Cariboo country. In a country of small rainfall, it takes years to grow a real man-sized tree and a great percentage of the fir timber that is at all handy to any kind of transportation will probably be gone in the next twenty years.

If the great moguls of the timber industry could ever whittle up their brains good enough and come alive with some sort of use for our jack-pine timber, there would be enough to support a whole pile of folks and the country for many, many years. But to date, outside of fence rails, log fences and log cabins and firewood, it has no value.

In the fall of 1951 I went down to Vancouver for a few days and stopped with my old friend, Mr. Harrison, and his family, and really enjoyed their never-failing hospitality and kindness.

The year of 1952 came drifting along and my son, Ronnie and I decided to buy a smaller ranch on the Fraser, which was a fairly productive little spot with a lot of possibilities added. But a few weeks after we made this deal, along came the foot-and-mouth disease in some prairie cattle brought in by a German emigrant who was working on a farm back there.

Well, sir, this sure did raise hell and set a chip under it. All the cattlemen including my son and I, suffered as the bottom dropped out of the cattle market and a lot of cattle were sold in the fall of 1952 for half price or less and this made it a very rough deal for us.

To climax matters, Peg at Big Bar Lake, had a terrible fire at her guest ranch. It burned the layout right down to the ground, and, of course, with very little insurance on it, the problem of getting started up again was a rough one for her. However, Peg has a great heart and a never-say-die character, and a month or so after the fire she started to try and rebuild the lodge, which, after a lot of worry, hard work and effort she managed to get done. I have always hated the year 1952 as it proved to be, for me anyway, the worst year in all my years in our Cariboo. It beats hell how a fellow can go along, seemingly all right, when all of a sudden, something comes along the trail that just jolts him in the rear end, like a real old cyclone.

The following year I lost my old friend and associate, Mr. Harrison, who died in his sleep at his home. I went down with a heavy heart to help carry him out to his last resting place.

I sure loved the old "General" and his many colourful characteristics, the great drive he always had, the homespun philosophy and the understanding heart which was always present with him, will be forever remembered by this old cowboy.

My son, Ronnie, got married to a very nice little gal from the coast in the spring of 1954, which made things a lot more comfortable and homelike down on that river, and Mary has turned out to be a real ranch girl and a great help to Ronnie.

The days and years seemed to fly by now, and with a lot more physical misery for me from a real dirty jack-pot that I got into down on that river. I was riding along on what I thought was a pretty gentle old sorrel mare in early 1955, and coming to a small creek in a gulch below the house on the river, I stopped to let my saddle mare have a drink of water. I was sitting kind of loose in my saddle, letting the mare drink when something must have scared her, because she jumped and whirled up out of the creek, and let right into bucking to beat hell, and with me not expecting anything like that. I was caught plumb out of line, and got bucked off the old mare, high, wide and handsome, and I lit on the rocks, striking my old head a real ringer on some rough-looking rocks lying in the gulch. It sure happened quick and dirty. I laid there on the ground for a little bit, kind of half knocked out, but I staggered up the gulch and was lucky enough to catch the old mare, who had got her feet tangled up in my bridle reins, and led her down to the barn which was a little ways away.

The final finish of this mix-up was that I had to get operated on in Vancouver and get two blood clots out of my old head, which looked like they were going to take me over the High Mountain.

This mess was just a forerunner of what followed me up later, arthritis in my old hands and feet, which really did put me in a rough position, then next on the list I had another rough run with pneumonia and oxygen tents, and all the trimmings. I came back out of that one so darned weak and worn out, I'd pretty near have to stand up twice to make a shadow.

This all just put me in a shape that I wasn't much use to myself, or anyone else either, and it worried me as I'd always been proud of being an active and energetic operator. Nowadays I'm more or less an old back-number, once in awhile doing some odd light jobs that come along. I spend most of my days living with my son on his little ranch on the river and once in awhile I'll go up to Big Bar Lake and visit around with old friends.

Approaching awful close to the seventy-year mark now, with so many of my old tillicums gone over across the mountain, I sometimes feel kind of lonesome, and wonder just how many more sheets I'll have to tear off the calendar before I head out to join them, which just don't perturb me one little bit, because I figure if a fellow's been all right here and tried to play the game, it would look like he should be all right there, wherever that may be.

When you get old, you wake up and find you've had quite a run and get into a habit of looking back at a lot of memories that drift across the mind. I gaze across the ocean of the past and find I have a long list of them, most of them all being pleasant and of a considerable variety, and I sure wouldn't take a million for them.

I had made a host of real worthwhile friends in all my years ranging all the way from the poor, but decent old Indian in his reserve, to outstanding leaders of industry in British Columbia. In my small way, I figure I have contributed to the progress made by our cattlemen and the honest-to-goodness, down-to-earth folks of our Big Bar country. I always sort of figure that at the end of our trail, it's not so much how much money and stocks and bonds you have that counts up, it's what you've done with your time that counts most, as the only thing we are ever remembered and respected for is our record.

Today our Cariboo, with good roads, truck lines and an up-to-date railroad and modern ways of living, have completely changed the picture, compared to the old pioneer days. The radio itself, being one of the most popular riggings that ever came into the country, bringing news and information that took days and weeks to arrive in former years. Our country has become a vast, impressive playground for the city dwellers, many of whom now own summer homes where they can relax from the city's turbulent grind and recharge their mental and physical batteries. Our country is changing in many different ways, but the spirit of our old pioneers and their children remains unaltered, and the wide ranges will be ever changeless.

I salute you, you old-timers, and I am more than proud to have been one of your tillicums, for in our Cariboo lies my heart.